FLEE · BE SILENT · PRAY

"This book will challenge and change you. It will require things of you that you may not think you are capable of, but in the end you will have discovered that, instead of a typical how-to book, you have encountered a written icon: a window into God, allowing for deeper intimacy and understanding."
—**TARA OWENS**, author of *Embracing the Body* and *At Play in God's Creation*

"Ed Cyzewski is reaching back into the history of Christian practice to recover a contemplative tradition. If you're looking for a still point in our turning world—the silence at the heart of faithful action—you should read this book."
—**JONATHAN WILSON-HARTGROVE**, author of *Reconstructing the Gospel*

"Too many believers lose faith when confronted with the silence, solitude, and mystery of death and suffering, especially believers who have an expectation that faith must involve words, certainties, and forward movement. In *Flee, Be Silent, Pray*, Ed Cyzewski introduces us to a God who dwells in the sanctuary of solitude, and he shares practices that enable us to do the same. This is a book that gives space for believers who need more than answers and certainties. This is a book for believers who want to find the presence of God in both life and death."
—**CALEB WILDE**, author of *Confessions of a Funeral Director*

"With gentle and hard-won wisdom, Ed Cyzewski opens our eyes to the ways our culture—both the secular and the

Christian—has created 'raw materials for anxiety production.' He is a compassionate guide, giving voice to fears that he has wrestled with. Ed's book reminds me that the search for God is full of distractions and that a contemplative life means consistently reorienting my posture toward God. But 'flee, be silent, and pray' are not words that encourage us hide from darkness. Instead, they are contemplative practices that—when followed—reveal God's presence with us in both the suffering and joy of the world. Ed's offering to anxious Christians is beautifully simple: ancient paths that reveal and heal."

—**CHRISTIANA N. PETERSON**, author of *Mystics and Misfits*

"I hope evangelicals discover the contemplative prayer practices that Ed Cyzewski introduces in this fine book and incorporate them into their lives. I hope they introduce these practices into their churches and make those churches stronger as a result. This hope is why I was penciling "Yes!" in the margins throughout *Flee, Be Silent, Pray. . . . Flee, Be Silent, Pray* is like a toolkit of implements we all can use to shape our souls and change the world."

—**JON M. SWEENEY**, author of The Pope's Cat series, from foreword

FLEE

BE SILENT

PRAY

ANCIENT PRAYERS
FOR ANXIOUS CHRISTIANS

ED CYZEWSKI

HERALD
P R E S S

Harrisonburg, Virginia

Herald Press
PO Box 866, Harrisonburg, Virginia 22803
www.HeraldPress.com

Library of Congress Cataloging-in-Publication Data
Names: Cyzewski, Ed, 1979- author.
Title: Flee, be silent, pray : ancient prayers for anxious Christians / Ed Cyzewski.
Description: Harrisonburg : Herald Press, 2019. | Includes bibliographical
    references.
Identifiers: LCCN 2018044070| ISBN 9781513804262 (pbk.) |
    ISBN 9781513804316 (hardcover)
Subjects: LCSH: Contemplation. | Prayer--Christianity.
Classification: LCC BV5091.C7 C99 2019 | DDC 248.3/2--dc23 LC record
available at https://lccn.loc.gov/2018044070

FLEE, BE SILENT, PRAY
© 2019 by Ed Cyzewski
Released by Herald Press, Harrisonburg, Virginia 22803. 800-245-7894.
    All rights reserved.
Library of Congress Control Number: 2018044070
International Standard Book Number: 978-1-5138-0426-2 (paperback);
978-1-5138-0431-6 (hardback); 978-1-5138-0436-1 (ebook)
Printed in United States of America
Cover and interior design by Merrill Miller

Unless otherwise noted, Scripture text is quoted, with permission, from the
New Revised Standard Version, © 1989, Division of Christian Education of the
National Council of Churches of Christ in the United States of America.

Scripture quotations marked (NIV) are taken from the *Holy Bible, New
International Version*®, NIV®. Copyright © 1973, 1978, 1984, 2011 by Biblica,
Inc.™ Used by permission of Zondervan. All rights reserved worldwide. www
.zondervan.com The "NIV" and "New International Version" are trademarks
registered in the United States Patent and Trademark Office by Biblica, Inc.™

23 22 21 20 19   10 9 8 7 6 5 4 3 2 1

To the Writer's Room

Contents

Foreword

THERE COMES A TIME for many evangelical Christians when they begin to ponder the practices of other denominations and Christian traditions. What may have once been regarded as wrong, strange, or even heretical becomes a clandestine curiosity. This happened to me. Then it might snowball; it did for me. Pondering can turn to life-changing.

In my case, I became concerned with how leaders in my church answered (or didn't answer) certain questions about belief and justice. Doubt set in. Then someone told me to read Thomas Merton, then Francis of Assisi. Soon I met actual Catholics, for the first time, and found them to be faithful people who didn't need saving more than I did.

Each spiritual path is unique. I ultimately left the evangelical church and became Catholic; many others who find contemplative prayer, like Ed Cyzewski, stay. I hope evangelicals discover the contemplative prayer practices that Ed introduces in this fine book, and incorporate them into their lives. I hope they introduce these practices into their churches and make those churches stronger as a result. This hope is why I was penciling "Yes!" in the margins throughout *Flee, Be Silent, Pray*. It's why I cheered when I read Ed's descriptions of overcoming his anxieties of faith on his way to meeting a wider cloud of witnesses.

Ed taps into some of the very best of Christian ways of praying. The chapters not only are about words of prayer but also introduce us to practices such as silence, gentleness, intention, humor, and how to navigate dark nights of the soul. Ed finds new teachers. He looks, for instance, to Saint Teresa of Avila for advice. She's often unknown to Protestants, since she was a prominent figure in the Catholic Counter-Reformation. But she's no longer the enemy, and her *Interior Castle* has the power to lead anyone to deeper ways of understanding a relationship with God.

In his quest to deepen a life of prayer, Ed looks to more recent great teachers too—people like Merton, Henri Nouwen, Richard Rohr. All are marvelous. I would add a few others from the last century: Jean Vanier, founder of L'Arche communities, who teaches that honest prayer requires vulnerability; Wayne Teasdale, who wrote and taught about being a "monk in the world"; and Julia Greeley, a former slave who lived such a quiet, profound life of service and prayer that many people now want to declare her a modern saint.

We're all called to be saints, and we all have so much to learn, and to do. The time is short. *Flee, Be Silent, Pray* is like a toolkit of implements we all can use to shape our souls and change the world.

> —Jon M. Sweeney,
>   translator/editor of *Francis of Assisi in His Own Words*,
>   and author of *The Pope's Cat* series for children

Author's Preface

TWENTY YEARS AGO I could not have written this book. Had I encountered a book like this back then, I would have eagerly—and anxiously—warned you as a reader against the ideas in its pages. So in a sense I had to write this book, as I used to be the least likely person to advocate for what follows.

Twenty years ago, I was a zealous evangelical Christian. Having grown up in a toxic and restrictive Catholic parish that left me resentful toward the power wielded by the priests, I had converted to the Protestant branch of the faith in a Baptist church. As an evangelical committed to Bible study, I had very little by way of spiritual practices or methods at my disposal. In the aftermath of becoming Protestant, I made it a life goal to undermine Catholicism, which I viewed with anger, resentment, and suspicion. It didn't help that I was surrounded by evangelical voices that said Catholics aren't "real" Christians.

But then something happened: my evangelical faith, which appeared to be so certain and enduring, crumbled. I'll tell that story in more detail in this book. As I struggled to pray during those years, I started to dabble in the writings of contemporary Catholic authors as a kind of last resort for my faith. Long story short: although I was now a committed Protestant, I had to return to my Catholic roots to learn how to pray.

By immersing myself in the prayer tradition that is preserved in Catholicism (and also remains in other branches, such as the Eastern Orthodox Church), I found relief from some of the greatest weaknesses of the evangelical movement, particularly the anxiety that comes from worrying that I can never do enough for God or ever become holy enough for God. Evangelicals will travel across oceans to proclaim salvation by faith and the grace of God, but we generally lack spiritual practices that connect us with the transforming presence of God in daily life. When the promises of God on paper don't transfer to real life, many evangelicals swing between trying to live a holier life, on one hand, and crashing into a crisis of faith on the other. Our faith is an anxious one.

Although many events and individuals were involved in the revival of my faith, my initial dialogue with Catholic authors such as Brennan Manning, Henri Nouwen, Richard Rohr, and Thomas Merton provided a constructive and life-giving approach to daily spiritual practices that I have sorely needed. Manning and Nouwen were the first Catholic writers I found who introduced me to contemplation; my evangelical university seemed to deem them the "safe Catholics" to read. I later found Rohr and Merton, who then paved the way for authors such as Cynthia Bourgeault, Thomas Keating, Jeanne Guyon, and Teresa of Ávila. Through reading these authors, I was pleased to discover that contemplative prayer is open to all who wish to practice it and can bring great benefits in the search for God. Christians of all backgrounds who are anxious about reaching out to God or who struggle with spiritual practices can find a constructive path toward cultivating a daily attentiveness to God through contemplation. Evangelicals like me are particularly in need of this quiet, restful practice, which predates the canonization of the New Testament.

I want to make an important distinction at the outset between describing myself as an "anxious evangelical" and those who suffer from anxiety attacks or those with a generalized anxiety disorder. If you struggle with anxiety or have regular panic attacks, I don't want anything I write to suggest that you should not seek the care of a psychiatrist or psychologist. I know many people who have found health and peace by taking medication for their anxiety. Anxiety comes in many shapes and forms. My journey through anxiety, which stems in part from my anxious evangelical faith, is hardly a template for anyone else's. People suffering from anxiety should pursue the treatments and practices that they need.

Yet my one encouragement to those who have anxiety struggles is this: don't rule out the ways Christian spirituality can also help. We live in anxious times, and anxious religion—along with the current political climate in the United States—is hardly making things better. It's possible that religion hasn't helped you because you haven't been given the basic practices that have brought peace to previous generations. So just as I encourage everyone with anxiety to keep their medical and psychological treatment options open, I also encourage everyone to remain open to the ways that contemplative prayer can lead to greater spiritual and mental health over the long term.

I wouldn't be surprised if many of today's confident Christians eventually wind up with the affliction of spiritual anxiety that sent my own faith into a tailspin. In *Flee, Be Silent, Pray*, I offer my story of interacting with Catholic contemplative writers as a particularly suspicious Protestant. It is my greatest hope that readers will find a God who is more loving and present than they had ever suspected. When we flee, are silent, and pray, we have a chance to reconnect with a Christian tradition that lives and breathes because of God's sustaining presence.

ONE

Say Goodbye

Exiting the Anxiety Factory

I consider that the spiritual life is the life of man's real self, the life of that interior self whose flame is so often allowed to be smothered under the ashes of anxiety and futile concern.

—THOMAS MERTON

CHRISTIANITY IN AMERICA today is often an anxiety factory. Can we ever do enough for Jesus? We can always pray more, serve more, evangelize more, read the Bible more, and grow more into Christ's likeness. Words like *discipleship* and *obedience* carry connotations of trying harder, doing more, and always bumping one's personal commitment up another notch. Christians might affirm "faith alone" in theory, but we also worry that faith is not sufficient. Praying and serving and sharing the gospel and reading Scripture are good things in themselves, so the anxiety we feel about abounding in these practices may be tolerated as a holy anxiety, of sorts. But it's anxiety nonetheless.

Our spiritual lives become like shareholder meetings, during which we need to demonstrate increases in profit and potential gains in the next quarter. We might believe we are saved by grace, but when it comes to actually living like Christians, we spend years struggling to pray, failing to meet the standards of our faith, and wondering if we have somehow been abandoned by God. Some of us might even begin to fear that all our efforts to reach a seemingly silent God mean that God is an illusion.

My own evangelical Christian tribe is particularly adept at manufacturing anxiety. Evangelicalism is a religious stream that grew out of a genuine desire to experience God, but it can also produce a state of spiritual uncertainty and even misery.

As a dominant branch of Protestant Christianity, evangelicalism focuses on Christ's saving work on the cross, a high regard for the Bible, the belief that all humans need to be saved, and the call to Christians to share the gospel. Fulfilling all these goals can become even more anxiety-producing when cultural and political priorities get tossed into the mix. Evangelicalism has been the primary tradition of Christianity that impacted my spiritual journey, and it will come up often when describing the anxiety present in Christianity today. However, the shift from anxious faith to the grounding of contemplative prayer is surely relevant for Christians from other traditions as well.

Evangelicals have often tried to prove themselves as spiritual insiders worthy of God's love, and plenty of other Christians who don't bear the evangelical label have dabbled with similar attempts to prove themselves worthy of God. However, evangelicals take this a step further by focusing on foundations, systems, interpretations, beliefs, and other boundaries that define who we are and who doesn't belong with us. We are so eager to be on fire for God, to make extreme sacrifices for God, and to prove (although without using the word *prove*) that we are worthy of Jesus' ultimate sacrifice on the cross. If Jesus gave his life for us, don't we owe him the same thing? If Jesus gave us a job to do, shouldn't we hop to it without delay?

Evangelicals are good at caring about causes. A cause can be a good thing, but when a cause is married to religious performance or a falsely spiritualized identity, it can create a perfect storm: anxious religious people trying to outdo each other in their commitment.

So is it any surprise that contentious factions in the church are all convinced of their own doctrinal and activist purity and then fearfully defend them? Fears of failing as a Christian, fears of apathy about important causes, fears about the decline of church attendance, fears about contemporary culture wars and the need to defend a particular theology or doctrine—add up all these fears, and you've got great raw materials for anxiety production.

As I've grown aware of my own struggles with anxiety, the nature of our anxious times becomes clearer as well. I spend each day surrounded by endless supplies of anxiety—and our family doesn't even own a television. When I told a friend that I was working on this book, she replied, "Could you hurry it up?" In fairness, there are plenty of concerning and troubling items in our news that conscientious people must learn about in order to live responsibly in their communities. But anxiety and fear are also powerful forces that are ruthlessly employed on ratings-hungry news shows and social media. Although the creators of anxiety-provoking media content bear their fair share of blame for inspiring fear and dread in their followers, our own agency in managing this anxiety is easy to overlook. Thomas Merton wrote, "Ours is a time of anxiety because we have willed it to be so. Our anxiety is not imposed on us by force from outside. We impose it on our world and upon one another from within ourselves."[1]

I suspect that sometimes our minds are so distracted and anxious that we can't fully grasp just how distracted and anxious we truly are. When anxiety and fear become our default ways of relating to the world, we run the risk of forgetting that there are other ways to approach each day and to process the thoughts and emotions that come streaming into our minds. Even stepping outside of our cultural anxiety is counter-intuitive and countercultural. The desert father Abba Anthony once remarked, "A time is coming when men will go mad, and when they see someone who is not mad, they will attack him, saying, 'You are mad; you are not like us.'"[2]

If our culture has normalized fear and anxiety, then it shouldn't surprise us that this anxiety and uneasiness will be manifested in our spirituality. Our hardworking, goal-oriented society is bound to latch onto the aspects of religion that measure progress, worry about not doing enough, and fear the evaluation of a superior if those goals aren't met.

Many Christians today, especially evangelicals, have lacked the practices of the historic church that lead to peace and communion with God. But fear not. The path to peace with God is closer than you can imagine. The Christian prayer tradition offers us this hope: anxious Christians can escape their current anxiety entrapment and become aware of God's loving presence with three deceptively simple practices: Flee. Be silent. Pray.

Author Henri Nouwen writes that these three actions—flee, be silent, pray—form the basis of the contemplative prayer tradition that blossomed to life with the desert fathers and mothers.[3] Nouwen shares the story of Abba Arsenius, who left his high status as a senator in ancient Rome in order to seek God in the desert. When Abba Arsenius prayed, "Lord, lead me in the way of salvation," he heard a voice say, "Arsenius, flee, be silent, pray always, for these are the sources of sinlessness."

Flee? Be silent? Pray? If those three words sum up the contemplative tradition, they are just about the opposite of my evangelical mandate: Engage! Speak up! Read Scripture! Fleeing the world feels like a defeat for the great commission, and silence will hardly do for those who imagine that being salt and light requires speaking up. Evangelicals—at least white middle-class ones—see themselves as active or even prominent members of the public square shaping culture and policy, broadcasting their teachings in many mediums, and countering secular institutions with their own biblically based counterparts.

Flee? Be silent? Pray? Can you imagine an evangelical church, school, or institution incorporating these three elements into its foundational mission, vision, values, beliefs, and staff manuals? I'm pretty sure this would be written off as madness. And if you read some of the stories about the desert fathers and mothers who sought God in the deserts of Egypt and Palestine around AD 300–400, you might be tempted to write *them* off as crazy extremists.

Yet the spiritual legacy of this isolated and silent movement continued for centuries throughout the Western church until it became largely confined to monasteries during the Reformation and Counter-Reformation. It was never lost in quite the same way in the Eastern Orthodox Church.

Flee, be silent, pray: all work together as one intentional movement toward God. The pursuit of God in silent, contemplative prayer is the exact opposite of anxious striving, studying, and cultural crusading. Contemplative prayer is the only cure I know for our holy anxiety and perceived alienation from God, because it places all our faith in the love and mercy of God.

WHAT IS CONTEMPLATIVE PRAYER?

Contemplative prayer is the intimate experience of God within us. It begins with a simple intention to be present for our loving God and trusts God's indwelling Holy Spirit will do the work of prayer and transformation within us. Contemplative prayer is often described as a time of waiting on the Lord (Psalm 27:14) and turning our eyes upon Jesus (Hebrews 12:1-2). Contemplative prayer is also described as a pure gift from God, but certain spiritual practices can help us receive that gift rather than remain unaware of it. We might think of these practices as preparing the ground for what God will plant and cause to grow in us through contemplative prayer. These practices could be silence, centering prayer, *lectio divina*, the Examen, or meditating on the Psalms, although there are many variations of these that go by different names.

Contemplative prayer tells us that we can't add anything to what we already have in Christ. We can't do anything different to make God love us more, and we probably need to buy and own fewer things in order to minimize our distractions. Contemplation is about doing less so that God can do more. We aren't getting ourselves out of the way in order to become nothing. We're getting our distractions out of the way in order to experience the "something" of God—even if that "something" sometimes feels like "nothing."

The practice of contemplative prayer is older than the New Testament canon. It dates back to the early church and runs through many streams of Christianity to this day. While the Eastern Orthodox Church has practiced contemplation in part through the recitation of the Jesus Prayer ("Lord Jesus Christ, Son of God, have mercy on me, a sinner"), contemplative prayer took up various forms in Western monasteries. The form of contemplation that many Western churches use traces back to the fourteenth-century book *The Cloud of Unknowing*. This prayer guide was written by an anonymous monk in England who advised his novices to use a single prayer word to recenter their attention on God's presence and to then let their simple desire of love for God pierce the cloud of unknowing that hid God from them. Each wave of monastic reform in the history of the church has relied on the prayer traditions of the desert fathers and mothers, cultivating daily contemplative practices so that God could grow new life in that space.

The contemplative writers who have helped me the most are Catholics—the group I spent the early years of my faith trying to discredit and dismantle. I'm still a Protestant's Protestant (Reformation Day is my spiritual Fourth of July). But it took humbling myself under the teachings of Catholic authors like Henri Nouwen to finally find the peace of God that had long eluded me.

Even the Catholics themselves tried to kill or censure mystics and contemplative teachers at times, often settling for imprisoning them and burning their books. In the 1500s Catholic authorities neglected the more mystical parts of the spiritual exercises of Saint Ignatius because those elements weren't intellectual enough. Saint John of the Cross was imprisoned by rival Carmelite monks because his monastic rule was deemed by some to be too strict. Many of the writings of the Catholic mystics gained a wider following only after their deaths. The mystics themselves were often unable to share their books, which empowered people to experience God outside the authority structure of the church. Mysticism became associated with frowned-upon spiritual experiences that authorities could not control. Meanwhile, the early Protestant Reformers saw the whole lot of Catholicism and decided to just not go there. They contented themselves with translating the Bible and burning each other at the stake over theological disagreements. Whether disliked, feared, neglected, or a mix of all three, contemplative prayer went from being *the* way to pray to being a prayer practice largely restricted to the monasteries, at least in the Western church.

As I said, while the contemplative tradition appears in several different camps of Christianity today, I have found the most life through the writings of Catholic contemplatives. But I turned to their works kicking and screaming, choosing them only as a last resort when my evangelical faith crashed. Ironically, while evangelicals have worked hard to distinguish themselves from Catholics by suggesting that we follow a more culturally aware and spiritually accessible path to God, many aspects of our movement make us prime candidates for practicing contemplative prayer. Even if you're a Christian who doesn't identify as an evangelical Christian, perhaps you'll see glimpses of the roots of your own holy anxiety by taking a brief peek at the composition of the evangelical movement.

WHO ARE EVANGELICALS AND WHY ARE THEY SUSPICIOUS OF CONTEMPLATION?

Evangelicals are a diverse, complex, and sometimes contradictory bunch. We claim to have peace with God, yet most of us know very little of the spiritual practices the historic church used to find such peace. When I discussed the concept of this book with my evangelical friends, nearly all of them laughed knowingly, if not a little nervously. They knew exactly what it feels like to be promised God's peace—and then to be left adrift, feeling far from God while trying to prove themselves spiritually without a clear path forward. I know such feelings are not confined to evangelicals, but they certainly are common within our camp.

The white evangelical Christian movement in the United States has largely settled for a fortress mentality, set on defending doctrines, institutions, and cultural influence. Some would even say that evangelicalism produces anxiety because it is derived from a series of reactionary, defensive movements. In many ways, the evangelical identity of many in America has become a fearful false self, which stands uneasily on a foundation of biblical knowledge, cultural influence, and entrepreneurial leaders. (For the sake of clarity: the American strain of evangelicalism shouldn't be confused with the whole of the global movement. While many similar emphases on Scripture, salvation, and evangelism can be observed in evangelical congregations in Asia, Africa, Latin America, and more diverse evangelical congregations in the United States, I'm speaking here of dominant evangelicalism in America.) Digging back to the roots of our movement, however, we can find an intriguing possibility for evangelicals who seek peace through the practice of contemplative prayer.

Evangelicalism grew out of the pietism in Europe during the 1600s that pursued a personal relationship with God despite the objections of many Protestants at the time. In addition, throughout the 1500s and 1600s, the Roman Catholic Church had its own inquisitions, inquiries, and persecutions against mystics who advocated for personal union with God. Speaking very simply about the early days of the evangelical movement, the Pietists had spiritual freedom, but they lacked the spiritual form and structure of the contemplative tradition. Meanwhile, the Catholics lacked the freedom to make their spiritual practices widely available. It's striking to think of what the church could have become, in the West at least, if these two groups had been allowed to flourish and even intersect.

Evangelist John Wesley discovered the confident, personal spirituality of the Pietists while traveling with a group of Moravians. He merged this personal pursuit of God's presence with the structure of his Holy Club, a Bible study, prayer, and service group. Richard Rohr has noted that Wesley was close to contemplative practice but lacked the teaching that would have schooled him in it. Such contemplative practices and teachings would have been mostly restricted to monasteries and convents at the time in the Western church. The evangelical movement has been largely driven by pious men and women who were deeply committed to prayer, even if they lacked instruction or direction from those connected to the ancient Christian practices of contemplation.

The stories of prayer as a driver of the activism and outreach of evangelicals are many and varied. The Britain-based evangelist George Müeller exhibited an astounding faith in God's provision for his orphanage, trusting God for his daily needs sometimes down to the last minute. The American missions movement, which first identified itself as the "Haystack Movement," has been traced back in part to a small prayer meeting in the 1800s that relocated to a haystack because of a thunderstorm. Billy Graham spent his early years taking long walks in order to seek God's direction. When Graham's ministry hit a decisive turning point, with an opportunity to broadcast his sermons on the radio, he dropped to his knees and trusted the outcome to God's provision while representatives from the radio station waited impatiently.

With the lure of political power, our attachment to cultural influence, the appeal of simple theological categories, and the sentimentality of preserving our institutions even if their leaders commit grievous sins, it shouldn't surprise us to see our unstructured heritage of prayer slip away. Members of the evangelical movement know they should pray, and they want the benefits of prayer. But when Christians who lack spiritual roots sit down to actually pray, they simply aren't sure what to do other than ask God for things. I excelled at asking God for things, but for most of my life I knew very little about resting in the loving presence of God.

It also shouldn't surprise anyone that many Christians, not just evangelicals, struggle to focus on prayer because of distracting or "afflictive" thoughts. When I began writing publicly about contemplative prayer, I asked my readers to name their greatest distraction in prayer. This wasn't multiple choice; it was a simple, open-ended question. I expected to receive answers all over the board that I could address on my website over the course of a few months. Instead I received more than six hundred replies, and nearly 90 percent mentioned the same exact struggle: distracting thoughts. Many of the spiritual practices and approaches to contemplative prayer are more or less designed to help us face our thoughts, surrender them to God, and wait on God in silence.

The "restfulness" of contemplative prayer has felt like the kind of Christian spirituality I longed for as an anxious evangelical, a deep longing that could never find fulfillment. It feels as if I finally have a place for God in my soul. Nevertheless, no matter how much my soul may long for resting in God, I frequently struggle to reach that point. In general, evangelicals in America—and plenty of Christians in other camps—are not good at resting, period. Contemplative prayer runs against our cultural and religious experiences and expectations.

Gloomy as that may seem, the dialogue of evangelicals and Catholics in the 1960s and 1970s gave many of us the gift of contemplative prayer once again. I personally benefited from this dialogue in the late 1990s when my evangelical university courses included books by Brennan Manning and Henri Nouwen. Books such as *Abba's Child* and *In the Name of Jesus* weren't just read and resold to the school bookstore. We underlined these books, discussed them, carried them around, and then clung to them years later.

Prayer has served as a foundation at key moments of the evangelical movement. But that passion for God has lacked the support of concrete spiritual practices that offer a long-term structure to hold that passion in place. Evangelicals have had little by way of daily spiritual practices to pass on from one generation to another, save for our commitment to make prayer requests and to study the Bible. Our lack of spiritual structure has left most of us to make up prayer as we go. We've been known to mimic one another at times with our earnest "Lord, we just . . . um . . . " and "Father God, we just . . . " prayers.

Some evangelicals get anxious at the mention of contemplative prayer. *Isn't that Catholic or Eastern Orthodox? Isn't that Buddhist? Isn't that a slippery slope into New Age religion?* Many of us are terrified of slippery slopes. One minute you're doing a downward dog stretch in a yoga studio and the next minute "Eastern religion" has taken hold. Next thing you know, you're moving furniture to make space for a shrine in your living room. We've all heard that this happened once to a friend of a friend of someone we knew at a church somewhere.

Evangelicals are so anxious about losing our faith that we're even afraid of other Christian traditions, which can somehow "feel" like a different religion. Tragically, these Christian traditions, such as Catholicism, have the potential to offer a resolution to the struggles and worries of evangelicals.

Contemplative prayer can be particularly intimidating for evangelicals who are addicted to doing things. We gravitate toward solutions that revolve around Bible reading plans, spiritualized organization systems, or outreach workshops and strategies. We want progress and growth by acquisition in our consumer-based faith. Many of us have little use for spiritual practices that involve seeking solitude, sitting still, saying nothing, and trusting God to work in unseen ways. These trends show up in many strains of American religion, but evangelicals have inadvertently taken many American tendencies to their logical extremes when applied to a religious faith.

BURNING OUT, CRASHING HARD

I grew up under the suffocating teaching of controlling Catholic priests. I write more about that experience in chapter 3. For now I'll just say that as a teenager, when I left the Catholic Church, I thought I found freedom in the Wild West of evangelicalism. The music was better, the people appeared happier, and I didn't have a priest telling me how to read the Bible. Evangelicals did all kinds of great things, from fighting culture wars to serving people in need. We studied more, worshiped more, and served more than anyone else.

During those years I threw myself into service, mission, Scripture study, activism, and any other evangelical endeavor presented as authentic action for the truly committed. No matter how ineffective my work appeared, how much I struggled to become "pure" and "holy," or how much I endeavored to be an influential culture warrior, I failed to ask if my foundational beliefs and practices were problematic. Looking back now, I see that I made the mistake of trying to transform culture without first being transformed into someone worth imitating or able to offer something truly transformative.

Eventually, the fire of fighting spiritual battles faded for me, and the pursuit of God became deeply frustrating. I was left with only the hollow shell of my arguments and fears, and I lacked the substance of connection, let alone union, with God.

Even worse, Christianity has no shortage of religious-sounding pursuits and practices that may strengthen group loyalty or promote a false identity of self but will do very little to actually make people aware of God's loving presence. I couldn't introduce anyone to the love of God because I was so busy defending my faith and butting into conversations with my own religious agenda and arguments based on Scripture. Remember, the unofficial mantra of evangelicals is Engage, Speak Up, Read Scripture. Compassion for others could be reasoned away by the urgency of the gospel message and my own righteousness before God.

My evangelical anxiety peaked while in seminary. I suspect that I had a virtually limitless source of material to feed my anxiety by that point. When I immersed myself in even greater depths of evangelicalism in seminary, I burned out and crashed hard. At the end of my coursework I dropped my seminary diploma onto a dusty pile of theology books and realized that I had no idea how to pray. In retrospect, I realize now that I didn't even know if God existed, and I wondered if past "spiritual experiences" were just emotional moments. I could exegete Scripture in the original languages, but I didn't have words to pray. (Little did I know I wouldn't need many anyway.)

After graduating from seminary, I was exhorted by eager evangelical friends to attend peppy worship services and outreach events. The evangelical solution remained: do more things, say more words, and read more Scripture. I had nothing left for God—if there was any God—and I felt entirely empty.

Then one day a pastor I knew from one of my seminary classes invited me to his new prayer service. This was back when all the cutting-edge evangelicals were experimenting with liturgy, candles, prayer books, and in the extreme cases, art. In the worst-case scenario, some also added incense into the mix. This pastor didn't strike me as the type to jump on a trend. I think he genuinely wanted to figure out ways to make church meetings more meaningful and to provide a deeper connection with God. Reluctantly, I agreed to show up.

Liturgy, chants, and candles were the last thing that I, as a former Catholic, wanted out of church. But I was desperate to prove to myself that I was still a Christian and to prove to myself that God is real. If anything, attending the service felt like a huge step backward. Evangelicalism was supposed to be my savior, the thing that rescued me from the seemingly lifeless liturgy of my Catholic days.

But the whole service was completely unlike anything I had experienced as either a Catholic or an evangelical. We chanted about God's love. We spent time centering on the Jesus Prayer. We meditated on Scripture using the slow reading practice known as *lectio divina*, which helped us pray the words of Scripture. Throughout the service I kept worrying that I was doing it wrong and wondering why I wasn't having an encounter with God. It didn't seem to be working. Either I was hopelessly broken or God wasn't real. I returned home defeated, and I plunged deeper into my spiritual despair.

Yet in the following days I found myself returning to those prayer practices, just in case. Little did I know that this pastor had sown the seeds for my spiritual liberation from my anxious, hardworking evangelical tradition. The practices in this underwhelming service would transform my faith, help me learn how to pray again, and allow me to rediscover the love of God.

PRACTICING THE PRACTICE

The intent of this book is to provide anxious Christians with a starting point for contemplative prayer and related spiritual practices, and it especially addresses many of the typical barriers that Christians face with regard to contemplation. Grounding the book in my own story of discovering contemplation means I particularly address hang-ups for prayer that conservative and evangelical Christians often face. This is not a definitive guide to contemplative prayer.

Writing about contemplative prayer as an evangelical gives me a particular advantage. Evangelicals have anxious spirituality nailed down, so if anyone can help anxious Christians work through their anxiety and its sources, it's evangelicals. In the chapters that follow, I share how I came to value contemplative prayer, and I then offer introductions to some of the practices that have helped me become aware of God's presence. At the end of each chapter, I provide a simple next step that will help you put something from the chapter into practice. You could say that it's a bit like an application point at the end of a sermon. Or not.

Actually, I'd prefer not. But there you have it.

TWO

Start at Love

Learning What Jesus Knew

For me, prayer is an upward leap of the heart,
an untroubled glance towards heaven, a cry of
gratitude and love which I utter from the depths of
sorrow as well as from the heights of joy.
It has a supernatural grandeur which expands the
soul and unites it with God.

—THÉRÈSE OF LISIEUX

A **S I'VE CONFRONTED** fears and anxieties related to my faith, I've frequently returned to two verses. "There is no fear in love, but perfect love casts out fear" writes John in 1 John 4:18, and the apostle Paul writes in 2 Timothy 1:7 that "God did not give us a spirit of cowardice." (*Cowardice* is translated as "fear" in several Bible translations.)

If you are experiencing fear, especially fear of God, then you are not receiving something from God. If you are filled with fear, the most helpful way I've found to drive it out is to seek the love of God. While contemplative prayer and related spiritual practices aren't the only avenues for experiencing the love of God, contemplative prayer is one of the oldest and most reliable spiritual practices from the historic church. It has deepened the awareness of God's love for many of its practitioners.

The foundation of contemplative prayer isn't a matter of what I need to do or become. Instead of frustrating myself time and time again by trying to live differently, I need to be reoriented around the love of God. The simple biblical truth is that God is actively seeking you and me. God is already present, loving me just as I am, even when I believe I am unworthy, unsanctified, and distant from God. None of these things change God's love for me. God's love is preemptively with us before we try any new prayer practice. There isn't a spiritual height I need to reach to "unlock" or "earn" God's love and presence.

If that strikes you as a major stretch because of what you've been taught about sin or depravity, try asking, "What if?" What if God loves you right here and right now as you are? What if God is already among us, prepared to be present with you and me in prayer? Would that reality change how you pray and how you practice holiness? What if the many Scriptures about waiting on the Lord, about God's compassion and mercy, God's loving-kindness, and God's love for the world have been overshadowed or obscured?

Would it be so bad to believe that God is more loving and merciful than you suspected?

We need more than commands, teachings, and obligations to live fruitfully as Spirit-filled followers of Jesus. We need God's transforming love. Until we can pray, serve, and minister out of God's love, we'll forever struggle with anxiety about not doing enough for Jesus or losing something that we had to fight to gain. We need to know that there's a Parent who loves us unconditionally. Any transformation and holiness we experience proceed out of the peace and security of that love.

As an anxious evangelical, I wanted to see clear biblical proof that these practices come straight from Scripture. If I was really going to buy the contemplative approach to prayer that begins with a deep trust in God's present love, I needed the Bible to change my mind. Before I would fully trust the Catholic authors who were leading me into contemplative prayer, I turned to the Bible. When I started to look for the love of God in the gospel stories, I was shocked to see what I had overlooked for many, many years.

WHAT JESUS KNEW

The unconditional, parental love of God is precisely what Jesus communicated to us through his baptism and transfiguration. In these two pivotal moments of Jesus' ministry, anxious Christians will find more than enough hope.

What formed the foundation of Jesus' ministry? The beginning of his ministry (baptism) and the point at which he turned toward Jerusalem (transfiguration) were both preceded by identical statements from God the Father: "This is my Son, whom I love; with him I am well pleased."

> As soon as Jesus was baptized, he went up out of the water. At that moment heaven was opened, and he saw the Spirit of God descending like a dove and alighting on him. And a voice from heaven said, "This is my Son, whom I love; with him I am well pleased." (Matthew 3:16-17 NIV)

> While he was still speaking, a bright cloud covered them, and a voice from the cloud said, "This is my Son, whom I love; with him I am well pleased. Listen to him!" (Matthew 17:5 NIV)

It is easy to jump past these statements, just as it's easy to overlook how frequently Jesus set off to pray by himself. If Jesus is a member of the Trinity, we might ask, why did he need the affirmation of God? Why did he wake up early to pray, pull praying all-nighters, and venture into the abandoned wilderness?

To a certain degree, Jesus modeled what ministry and a relationship with God is supposed to look like. He was fully God and fully human, but he mysteriously manifested the power of God through his humanity. Paul writes: "In your relationships with one another, have the same mindset as Christ Jesus: Who, being in very nature God, did not consider equality with God something to be used to his own advantage; rather, he made himself nothing by taking the very nature of a servant, being made in human likeness" (Philippians 2:5-7 NIV). I'll leave the trinitarian particulars of Paul's statement to people who are smarter and better read than I am. What we can't avoid is the fact that Jesus ministered fully in human likeness and received the loving affirmation of God, who identified Jesus as his beloved Son at two pivotal moments in his ministry.

Before Jesus preached about the kingdom, healed the sick, or dined with the outcast, he received affirmation from God. Because of that affirmation, he had nothing to prove. His identity was secure, and there was nothing anyone could give to him or take away from him that mattered more than the loving affirmation of the Father. He was God's beloved Son, filled with love to share with those in need and to protect himself against the anger and criticism of others.

Jesus' love for others was ever present, empowering him to show compassion to the crowds who were tired, hungry, and needy, always asking for another miracle. His love extended to the quarrelsome Samaritan woman, who engaged in a theological debate in the heat of the day in order to mask her personal history. When his friends ran away, executioners drove nails into his body, and mockers shouted insults, Jesus gasped words of forgiveness. As Peter stood before him sopping wet, half naked, afraid, and ashamed of denying him, Jesus extended mercy and acceptance to his friend.

Where did this capacity for love come from? While I don't claim to know the deep mysteries of God, the Bible appears to point to the baptism and the transfiguration as essential high points in the ministry of Jesus. We ignore them at our peril. Here is God literally speaking words of love and affirmation for his Son.

If you've ever thought that hearing God speak from a cloud would help you figure out what to do with your life, that's exactly what God did for Jesus. It is amazing to think that God could have said anything at all to Jesus at the start of his ministry and before its final climax. Yet he chose to say, "This is my Son, whom I love; with him I am well pleased."

What would we expect God to say to us from a cloud? What would be so important that God would literally shout it from the sky? The anxious Christian's version of God's message would sound something like "Don't forget that the Bible is inerrant and fully inspired in all that it ordains and teaches!" or "You should have gone on that mission trip!" or "Why don't you pray more?" or "Don't ask any questions about the doctrine statement you signed at your church!" or "I hope you are having pure thoughts right now!" or "You better not be ashamed of sharing the gospel. Now what's your name again?" Christians from traditions other than evangelicalism may imagine other versions of this frustrated, disappointed God who just wishes we could get our act together.

The force of God's affirming love for Jesus may be lost on us. We assume that of *course* God loved Jesus, since Jesus is God and God loves God and of course God would like Godself—or however the Trinity works. But just as Jesus came to change what his listeners thought about the kingdom of God, Jesus also helped us redefine the love and acceptance of God. Jesus modeled a life grounded in the security of God's love. This preemptive love and affirmation introduces us to grace and to the pure gospel of God's loving care for us as our Creator. If we can grasp what God wants us to know through these interactions with Jesus, the rest of the Gospels make a lot more sense. God's single line for a beloved Son summarizes the parable of the prodigal son. Whether we have rebelled and run away or we have stayed behind and judged those who don't measure up, God the Father runs out to both of us. Both the rebellious and the self-righteous are being pursued by the parental love of God. Both have a place with the Father. And as a word of caution to those who believe they have earned God's approval through their religious practices, those who are willing to confess their failures are more likely to recognize the love of God.

We could even say that Jesus' love was so large that it ultimately led to his execution. Jesus offended so many different people in his audience because he showed the same radical love and acceptance to every single person. He loved and accepted Samaritans, tax collectors, the sexually promiscuous, Pharisees, Roman soldiers, common laborers, and revolutionary religious zealots. He patiently answered the questions of the Pharisees, dined with the most notorious sinners, praised the faith of Roman soldiers who were aligned with pagan deities and particularly evil rulers, and ministered alongside the common people and revolutionaries. Wealthy women and hardscrabble fishermen supported him and traveled with him. The love of Jesus was large enough for every political group, religious faction, and socioeconomic class.

You could take him or leave him. Regardless of how you responded, Jesus' love was large enough that he remained secure in his identity and ministry despite widespread rejection and hatred among his own people—even his own family. If you changed your mind about him, he always had an open invitation for you to return. The largeness of his love begins with the expansive love of God the Father, which affirmed him right from the start and continued into his ministry's darkest hours. Jesus gives to us what he has received from the Father, and what the Father expects us to do: extend to others what Jesus has given to us.

A spiritual principle emerges from Jesus' teachings: we can only give what we have received. We cannot give grace to others unless we have been shown grace first. This is at the heart of Jesus' parables, in which those who have been forgiven much are able to extend the same forgiveness to others. The most wicked are those who receive mercy and then fail to show it to others. Those who receive God's mercy are the ones who can extend mercy to others.

This is why Jesus described the life of God as a spring of water bubbling up within us. We aren't intended to be buckets or cisterns that store a limited amount of water, dispensing it sparingly to the select few. The life of God in us is an abundance that comes from God's healing presence in us rather than from our own efforts.

You don't become a bubbling spring of God's life through duty or study. You can only tap into the life of God by doing the "work" of abiding in the vine. The life of God takes care of itself in us as we connect with God. One way to abide in God's love is contemplative prayer, and it has proven essential for my own spiritual restoration.

You can walk the religious line or obliterate it. There is nothing you can do to become more unworthy or to make God love you more.

LIVING OUT OF LOVE

Let's assume that you have a mission to share the gospel of the kingdom. Let's assume that you've been sent to tell all people about the kingdom of God and that Jesus is alive today. What kind of training would you want for this mission? Better yet, what would you want God to shout at you from a cloud? What is the *one* thing you need to know above anything else? Could God say something in fifteen words or less (assuming God is speaking to you in New International Version English) that could change the course of history forever?

What if you were stepping out into ministry today and a cloud zipped up right over you, and the voice of God spoke to you by name:

You are my child . . .
Whom I love.
With you I am well pleased.

You haven't shared the gospel, served a meal, visited a prison, ministered to the sick, or supported a single heartbroken person through loss or tragedy. You haven't proven yourself worthy of anything. There is no success story to report, no growth to measure, and no testimony to celebrate in front of a crowd. Yet God is giving you the one and only thing that you need for your life and for your ministry.

If this one thing isn't good enough for you right now, nothing else will be good enough. You'll most likely spend the rest of your life burning out and living in fear that you're not worthy, that you're not doing enough, and that you'll never be able to draw near to God. If you aren't living out of the abundance of God's love for you, other people can become a threat to your accomplishments, doctrinal purity, and status. It's far safer to treat people who disagree with you as threats, dangers, and heretical outsiders. If you become the guardian of the gates, you become indispensable and powerful, protecting the right and wrong categories of religion. Decisions become cut-and-dried matters according to what's safe and what's a threat.

Without a foundation of God's love and acceptance, Christians are cut off from the capacity of God to love others generously and unconditionally. If we aren't declared God's beloved children on day one, and if we must perform in order to please God, then we had better work harder, debate theology endlessly, and worry that we have never done enough to merit God's acceptance and approval.

I could point you to plenty of Scripture passages about the love of God, such as Ephesians 3:17-19 (NIV): "I pray that you, being rooted and established in love, may have power, together with all the Lord's holy people, to grasp how wide and long and high and deep is the love of Christ, and to know this love that surpasses knowledge—that you may be filled to the measure of all the fullness of God." Yet it's one thing to believe that God's love defines God's interactions with us; it's quite another to actually accept that love of God for myself.

It's hard to sift through all the other things that the Bible says about God in order to figure out how they relate to God's love for us. These stories and doctrines of God—such as God's justice, holiness, and omnipotence—can begin to overshadow God's immeasurable love. Instead of being filled with this love to the measure of the fullness of God, we may end up being filled with fear of God or indifference toward a seemingly cold and ruthless deity. Even though Paul said that nothing can separate us from the love of God (see Romans 8:35-39), plenty of distractions and misconceptions can obscure it.

If there is one lifeline that I as an anxious evangelical have needed for prayer, it's the foundational truth that God's preemptive, unearned love for us forms the foundation of prayer. Some may even argue that God's love is essentially what prayer "is." Thomas Merton writes:

All desires but one can fail. The only desire that is infallibly fulfilled is the desire to be loved by God. We cannot desire this efficaciously without at the same time desiring to love Him, and the desire to love Him is a desire that cannot fail. Merely by desiring to love Him, we are beginning to do that which we desire. Freedom is perfect when no other love can impede our desire to love God. But if we love God for something less than Himself, we cherish a desire that can fail us. We run the risk of hating Him if we do not get what we hope for. It is lawful to love all things and to seek them, once they become means to the love of God. There is nothing we cannot ask of Him if we desire it in order that He may be more loved by ourselves or by other men.[1]

Even worse, our fears about God taint our ability to pray. Richard Rohr writes, "Most don't know how to surrender to God. How can we surrender unless we believe there is someone trustworthy out there to surrender to?"[2] The God I learned about for so many years in the evangelical fold wasn't a God worthy of devotion. This was a God who accepted me only because he figured out a loophole through the death of Jesus. This God was prepared to send me into the eternal flames of hell if Jesus hadn't intervened. It's no wonder I struggled to pray to this God. Why wouldn't I resort to formulas and simple supplications and rote words of praise? It's not that I was turned away by a God who didn't match my sensibilities and preferences. It's that I had missed the God whom Jesus revealed and shared with us. "Sinners in the hands of an angry God" is a far cry from "This is my Son, whom I love; with him I am well pleased."

If we allow ourselves to dwell with the words of Paul in Ephesians 3 for a moment, we may be surprised by the implications. First, we are rooted and established in love as our foundation. Love is our starting point. Is it a stretch to say that God is calling down from heaven to speak over us, "This is my child, whom I love; with you I am well pleased"? I don't think Paul would say that's a stretch at all. In fact, Paul makes the point that God's love isn't just our roots and our stability—God's love is what transforms us into the fullness of God. This is a love that surpasses our knowledge and extends into every conceivable direction. If we're going to take the Bible at its word, the love of God should continually shock us. If we are not routinely challenged in our knowledge and experience of God's love, then there's more to find today.

We dare not add or take away from the words of Scripture. This is the love of God that compelled Jesus to die and to rise again. This is the love that exists eternally among the Father, Son, and Spirit, and we are welcomed into this love as fully adopted children (see Ephesians 1:5). We have been chosen to partake in this preemptive love that has been extended to us before we could even think of ways to prove ourselves worthy.

BUT WHAT DO WE DO WITH ALL THAT ANXIETY?

So much of the anxiety among Christians, especially evangelicals, can be traced back to the ways we misconstrue, obstruct, or add conditions to the passionate love of God for us. Transformation always follows repentance, and transformation can take time—that seems to be the central message of the disciples' many failures in the Gospels. However, we won't begin to resemble Jesus unless we follow his same process of transformation and minister out of the same source of life. This is where the evangelical focus on the cross and atonement theories have taken our attention away from the life that Jesus modeled for us. Richard Rohr notes, "It seems that we Christians have been worshiping Jesus' journey instead of *doing* his journey."[3]

Contemplative prayer can be one way that we are filled to the full measure of the fullness of God. Most Christians have not been prepared to understand or experience the love of God in this personal, immediate way. As an evangelical, I learned about God's love as one doctrine among many to affirm, a fact to be grateful for, and something to reciprocate. God's love was something I could experience in theory, but devoting ten, twenty, or forty minutes a day to God's presence and love was far outside my experience. If anything, I was trained to be suspicious of anyone who makes too much of love; I thought such people were at risk of losing sight of the many boundary markers that defined a "faithful" Christian. Duty and devotion may prove motivating for a little while, but for many Christians, resting in God's love, quietly waiting on God's love, or patiently enduring the silence of a dark night of the soul sounds a bit off. The church fathers and mothers would certainly be astounded to see such a large segment of the church cut off from these practices and so fearful of even trying them.

Christians have been trained to be full of many things, but love is rarely one of them. As a result, we are anxious wrecks who prove ourselves as insiders if we are able to condemn the wrong people and to welcome the right people. We sign doctrinal statements and cut ourselves off from anyone who deviates from them. In much of my evangelical theology, God was often detached and mechanical. I struggled to pray because I couldn't imagine that the God I'd studied and tried to serve actually loved me. Was this God actively reaching out to me? Was this God willing to hear my prayers? As I struggled to pray, I assumed that either I'd messed things up beyond hope or God wasn't real. Some days it felt like a relief to not believe in that God.

The God I found in the writings of modern Catholic writers and the contemplatives from church history who influenced much of their writing revealed a very different kind of God. When I received God's love first instead of trying to earn it or prove myself worthy, I could finally find the freedom to pray and to experience God's transforming presence in my life. Jesus wasn't disappointed in me. If anything, he was the heartbroken lover longing for me to come back to him.

The Psalms tell us to wait patiently on the Lord. I used to read that as a kind of passive-aggressive move on God's part. Here I was, desperate for God, waiting and praying with all my heart. Would it kill God to show up when I pray?

Through contemplative prayer I have learned that I had everything completely backward. God has been waiting for us all along, but we are often too distracted, impatient, or fearful to meet with him. God's love is here and constant, and there is nothing I can do or feel to change that reality. I can ignore it or obstruct it, but I can't stop it. Learning to pray isn't about turning on the tap of God's love. Rather, learning to pray is about training ourselves to be present for the love of God that is already at work in our lives.

ACKNOWLEDGING GOD'S PRESENCE

Christian anxiety tells us that prayer isn't working because there must be something wrong with us. On the other hand, when we follow every imaginable rule and still come up empty, we conclude that the problem must be with God. Anxious prayers focus on results and progress, but God is more concerned about loving presence. Contemplative prayer has taught me that God's love is present and that I need only seek God in order to pray. I may have an epiphany, but I most likely will not. God's love is steady and constant, and many days I have to settle for taking that on faith. In fact, focusing on feelings and experiences has been my greatest barrier to contemplative prayer. I have had to completely shut down my anxious tendency toward measuring and proving my spiritual vitality and worth.

François Fénelon wrote, "How will you go on to maturity if you are always seeking the consolation of feeling the presence of God with you? To seek pleasure and to ignore the cross will not get you very far. You will soon be trapped in the pursuit of spiritual pleasures."[4] The journey into contemplative prayer calls on us to think differently of God and of ourselves. Very little depends on us. The spiritual "work" we do in contemplative prayer is very different from the spiritual labors of many Christians who are bogged down with lists of beliefs, practices, and activities necessary for pursuing holiness. As an anxious evangelical, I was never doing enough to win God's love or to achieve any kind of lasting life transformation. But how could we? God's love is already ours, and until we learn how to simply receive it, we'll remain in an anxious rut of performance, failure, and struggle.

The first step in many spiritual practices that we'll look at, such as the Examen and centering prayer, is a simple acknowledgment that God is present. That is so very different from my assumptions as an evangelical Christian who used phrases like "I'm waiting for God to show up." Theologically, I could affirm divine omnipresence. But practically I struggled to believe that

God was truly present with me and, most importantly, loving me right in that moment without preconditions.

Contemplative prayer took some practice and effort at first. I had to unlearn the anxious prayers of evangelical Christianity and to quiet my many thoughts and expectations. Along the way, I've found that contemplative prayer is less about what I do or the results I "experience." Contemplative prayer guides us toward resting in the fullness of God and God's love. It's a peaceful practice that pulls us away from striving, fear, and defending boundaries. As we learn to trust that God is present and we become even more aware of his loving presence, we'll begin to experience the transforming power of God in our lives.

You simply can't resist living with greater compassion and grace after experiencing the acceptance of God. This is the true prayer of a little child in the kingdom. If you can only call out, "Jesus, Jesus, Jesus," in faith and reliance, then you can pray. My own pride and hopes for spiritual advancement kept me from seeing how badly I needed to become like a little child in prayer.

In the chapters that follow, I'll share from my own meandering journey toward the present love of God and contemplative prayer in particular. I needed to learn several spiritual practices along the way that prepared me for "contemplative" practices, but they became essential aspects of my own path. Contemplative prayer is the gift of God's grace in our lives as we create space for God, and it can be nurtured through wordless prayer practices such as centering prayer and silence. That is the "flee, be silent, pray" part of this book.

To enter into prayer beyond words, however, I had to figure out what to do with all my thoughts and the words that came to mind while praying. Prayer practices such as the Examen and *lectio divina* prepared my mind for silence and contemplation, freeing me to direct my desires toward God's love without the distractions of my many thoughts. I share my own story not because I have excelled in any way more than others. I'm also by no means the first evangelical to find a home in contemplative prayer. But my shift toward contemplative prayer has been a dramatic one that demonstrates how anyone, even the most hostile skeptic, can benefit from it.

I went from being a Bible-thumping defender of the faith who viewed Catholics with anger and suspicion to a lover of Catholic authors and contemplative prayer practices. The way I view the Bible and prayer have changed dramatically over the years. The direction I didn't even know I was looking for was contemplative prayer. I suspect that may be the case for many other struggling evangelicals, not to mention Christians in other traditions.

Instead of providing a comprehensive guide to all things contemplative, I have chosen to limit the authors I cite to those who have proven pivotal at key points in my path toward contemplative prayer. I provide a list at the end of the book with further reading suggestions. Whether you enter into this book with a simple desire to pray more or because you feel that God has let you down, there is room for you in this loving search for God that begins with God's loving search for you.

Whether or not there's a dove or a cloud present, God is speaking a message of acceptance and grace for you in the midst of your daily work, relationships, and responsibilities. Surely the Lord has been with you and you did not realize it. Whether you need a booming voice from heaven to shake you free from your anxious thoughts or a gentle whisper to call you back to your first love, God is speaking to you right now in this place. This message is for you and you alone. It's the message you've been waiting for your entire life, even if you didn't know you needed it. It's a word that is stronger than death and is able to transform the hardest of hearts. If you want to step into the deeper experience of prayer and the peace of God, this is the lifeline that you will cling to day in and day out. It is the beginning and end of the Christian life. It is the message that keeps our world spinning and the sun rising anew each morning with fresh mercies settling like dew on the ground. This message is for you, if you can take it on faith, even right now:

You are my child, whom I love; with you I am well pleased.

Beloved, we have nothing to prove and everything to gain as we step into contemplative prayer together. May our fears and anxieties disintegrate as we experience the width and length and height and depth of God's love for us.

PRACTICING THE PRACTICE

What would God shout at you from a cloud?

No, really. Think about it. Would God be positive or negative? Encouraging or disappointed?

How does this imagined God affect how you pray? How does this image of God affect even your willingness to pray?

How would your views of prayer change if God audibly called, "You are my beloved child"?

THREE

Pray with Scripture

Moving from Defensive to Devotional Reading

*Satan's greatest psychological weapon is a gut-level feeling
of inferiority, inadequacy, and low self-worth. This feeling
shackles many Christians, in spite of wonderful spiritual
experiences . . . and knowledge of God's Word. Although
they understand their position as sons and daughters of
God, they are tied up in knots, bound by a terrible feeling
of inferiority, and chained to a deep sense of worthlessness.*

—DAVID SEAMANDS

IF YOU HAD BEEN searching for the evangelical Christian least likely to pursue contemplative prayer under the instruction of Catholic writers, I was the ideal candidate. I was a Bible-loving Protestant with a deep resentment toward the Catholic Church of my youth.

"The Bible can be really dangerous if you study it on your own," my priest told me when I was fifteen. The trouble was that I'd been reading the Bible on my own for three years and I was hooked. Most importantly, I believed that the Bible, especially Paul's letters, revealed serious errors in the Catholic Church, and this priest was trying to cover them up.

Like good Irish Catholics, my mother's family believed that I had to obey the priest if I wanted to remain Catholic. My grandfather, who lived three houses down from my mom, sided with that priest as well. There would be no Bible reading in their home, because the priest said so. My suspicions of the Catholic Church only grew as other priests at my Catholic school pressured me to stop reading the Bible and dismissed my questions. My parents were divorced, and since I couldn't see any way I'd give up reading the Bible, I decided to move in with my dad, who was Baptist.

I don't know if my family ever fully recovered from that decision. The two most important people in my life up to that point had been my mother and grandfather. After the day I moved out, we had no contact for weeks, and it would be six years until my mother and I could finally speak openly and safely with each other. The event that finally opened communication between us was the death of my grandfather. Although I reached out to him often and spent hours by his side as he suffered from cancer, he and I never had a chance to fully reconcile before he died. There were many reasons for our family's division during my high school years, but the number one cause, in my eyes, was the Catholic Church, especially my particular parish's obsession with preventing me from reading the Bible and the dismissive priests at my high school.

I don't want to oversimplify complex family events from my past. They remain some of my most painful memories, and a lot of things that happened before that explain why we all acted as we did. Yet I firmly believe that things didn't have to be this way. My curiosity about the Bible could have been nurtured and gently directed within the Catholic context. The priests were so afraid of the enchantments and errors of my dad's fundamentalist Baptist church that they adopted a scorched-earth approach. Ironically, by the time I moved in with my dad, he had already left that church in favor of an evangelical one that was far less combative toward Catholicism.

Once the priests advising my family set up an either/or situation, they created unnecessary pressure that squeezed me out of Catholicism. I blamed Catholicism as a whole—and the priests from my parish and high school in particular—for damaging many of my family relationships. Closed systems that thrive on control can't help but fail the people they claim to protect.

That is one lesson that I carried into seminary. Yet there I learned that even my beloved Bible could be used to establish closed systems of theology that restrict and alienate sincere students of Scripture in much the same way as the Catholic priests had done with me.

CAN YOU PROVE YOUR LOVE FOR THE BIBLE?

If the Catholic Church warned me not to take the Bible too seriously, seminary warned me constantly about not taking the Bible seriously enough. In seminary I crashed into theology debates and biblical interpretation battles that have raged for centuries. If I wanted my faith to survive, I needed to learn how to defend the Bible and my interpretations—and fast. I had learned to love the Bible, but once I immersed myself in a deeper study, it appeared to be something altogether different from what I had thought.

During seminary, the Bible that I had grown to love and study with the greatest of care became a fragile, contentious document for me. According to several of my professors, it was important to study the minute details of the chronology of the Hebrew kings or the events in the Gospels in order to prove that the Bible is completely true, reliable, and inerrant. Those who didn't wholeheartedly embrace this struggle for inerrancy were written off as having given up on the faith.

Even if I could prove that the Bible is 100 percent inerrant, there'd be no guarantee that I was interpreting it correctly. One small mistake and I could end up deceived and in danger of the fires of hell. And even if I were safe from the fires of hell, I could still be wrong about important things like baptism or the specific mechanics of salvation. I studied piles of theology books just to make sure I was in the "right" denomination—and that the people in my denomination were professing the correct truth. Theology debates weren't just academic exercises or rigorous exchanges of ideas between friends. In many cases, they turned into high-stakes missions to save each other from flawed theology that could put us on God's grumpy side or lead us down a slippery slope to hell.

While there were a few professors who fixated on defending the faith lest we lose it to atheists and liberals, I did have several irenic, gracious professors who could amicably disagree about the Bible and focused on preparing their students for ministry—which is rarely the same thing as apologetics. However, it was difficult to avoid the anxiety that had infected much of evangelical scholarship and had been passed on to seminary students who began to embody the wider trends of fear and defensiveness that have become the hallmarks of our religious subculture. Many students embraced the wider evangelical assumption in the air that you defend the Bible and your beliefs that are based on the Bible because that's what the Bible is here for. What else would you do with the Bible other than defend it?

Turning the Bible into a class textbook, of sorts, beat any passion for the Bible out of me. In my mind it became a fragile ancient manuscript that had to be meticulously dissected, protected, and defended lest the entire Christian faith collapse. I had entered seminary with a love for Bible study and a hope that ministry was the right career for me. By the time I took my diploma in hand, I didn't know what I thought of God or the Bible anymore. I didn't know what remained of my faith if I wasn't vigorously defending something from someone.

By trying to make the Bible true and relevant, I had lost the Bible. Now, on the other side of those days, I can see that I made the mistake of seeking life in the pages of Scripture rather than in Jesus himself. I hit a dead end with my faith, burning out spiritually and slipping into a crisis of faith. I couldn't find life by analyzing the theology in the pages of Scripture, and I had no idea how to pray. How does someone finish seminary and not know how to pray? I tried to attend church, but I kept slipping into theological defense mode every time we came to the Scripture readings or sermon.

It didn't matter if I could prove that the Bible was true when I didn't even know what to make of God or how to connect with God. After years of studying the Bible closely, I could hardly bring myself to read it. I didn't see the point anymore if God had abandoned me or simply wasn't real.

Around the time that my faith faltered in seminary, I had my first real anxiety attack. It occurred in part because of an evangelism class that required aggressively evangelizing strangers. A big part of being on fire for Jesus and committing to costly discipleship is sharing the gospel. In the anxious world of evangelicalism, "on fire" believers are supposed to be unashamed world-changers for Jesus. If you're not doing your part, then what's wrong with you?

We were given actual grades based on how well we shared the gospel. The class was taught by a kind, well-meaning Campus Crusade guy. A self-assured, extroverted evangelical, he believed that sharing the gospel with complete strangers was the most natural, normal thing anyone could do. While he could shift into a conversation about the eternal destination of one's soul while ordering a coffee at Starbucks, his version of evangelism made me completely unable to have normal conversations with people such as my car mechanic or the cashier at the supermarket. The panic attacks became more frequent. One day, as I gasped to breathe while in line at Walmart, I hoped to God—if God was even real—that there was a better way to share the love of God with others.

I barely passed the class. The weekly evangelism assignments just about destroyed me. I had to share the gospel with a stranger once a week for ten weeks and write a report on it. Perhaps some people reading this think that's no big deal. Surely others see that, for an introvert, pushing the gospel on unsuspecting people is the end of the world as we know it.

At the time I didn't connect the dots between all the different sources of anxiety in my Christian faith. Within my own evangelical tribe, I was surrounded by people exhorting me and my peers to defend the Bible, study the Bible, and boldly share our faith without shame. To rely on spiritual practices, to entertain doubt, or to back away from aggressive evangelism strategies was nothing short of failing the mission of Jesus. We were immersed in tests and trials that would prove whether we really were committed to God. The unspoken subtext in many situations was that our commitment would also determine God's acceptance of us. The defensiveness and expectations took their toll over time, and I ended up in the emergency room gasping for air. A nurse rolled her eyes at me. "Sir, you're having an anxiety attack," she said. "Go sit down and try to hold your breath!"

In truth, my soul was also gasping for air, seeking some other way to find God. I was clinging to a faint glimmer of hope that there must be another way forward without immersing myself in the vicious cycle of anxiety created by my beloved evangelical movement.

In the midst of my raging anxiety and disrupted faith, a conference call offered a glimmer of hope. That call became my first step toward a new understanding of Scripture and its role in my spiritual life. The Bible could serve as a guide to the presence of Jesus rather than as a repository of doctrines or a fortress of proof texts. My faltering faith could find the path to prayer that Christians have used for centuries in the book that had been right under my nose.

DEVOTION RATHER THAN DEFENSE

Phyllis Tickle was the most chipper, optimistic person I've ever spoken to on the phone. During a conference call, set up for our seminary class by an adjunct professor, she exuded warmth and cheer. She found "wonderful, wonderful" things to say about all the different Christian traditions during our talk about *The Divine Hours*, which she had recently finished editing. The series of three prayer books follows the church calendar and adapts the daily office, which includes Scripture readings (primarily from the Psalms) and prayers. The daily office is typically found in Catholic breviaries and the Anglican Book of Common Prayer. *The Divine Hours* organizes the daily office into three fixed-hour readings (morning, noon, and evening) and a brief compline (a service of evening prayers before retiring for the night).[1] There are short psalms, readings from the Gospels, Epistles, and Prophets, and a series of prayers that include a prayer based on the time of day and a prayer of the week.

As Tickle shared about the prayer heritage of the church, her optimism about Catholicism caught me completely off guard. Although a few charismatic Catholics from my days at an evangelical college occasionally threw my negative judgment of them into doubt, I still didn't see how anyone could gain much from such a closed and controlling system. Wasn't Catholicism more or less ruined by the authoritarian abuses of the priests and the other figures in power? Catholics weren't supposed to even read the Bible, right?

Phyllis Tickle saw things quite differently. She generously pulled from the Catholic liturgy of the hours and the Book of

Common Prayer, as well as several other prayer books. While *The Divine Hours* struck me as very Catholic—one prayer to Mary set off my theological alarms—these prayers offered an accessible on-ramp into slower, more restful prayer practices that didn't require a steady stream of my own words. Most of the Scripture readings were short and easily picked up for meditation throughout the day, with a collection of Scripture verses and prayers in each morning office, midday office, and evening vesper office. As I meditated on the selected verses each day, sometimes a single word or phrase stood out to me and offered a path forward in my prayers that day. That practice, in particular, proved immensely helpful when I learned more about contemplative prayer.

I had already attended a prayer service that had stretched me. In that service, led by a friend, we were encouraged to repeat the Jesus Prayer, to breathe deeply in silence, to light candles, and to chant. But Phyllis Tickle offered a more familiar path toward a different kind of devotional use of Scripture in prayer. While in Protestant contexts "devotions" usually means a kind of study that results in pages of journaling and reflection on the Bible with the hope of increasing one's knowledge of Scripture and landing on life-changing epiphanies, the divine hours encouraged me to stop looking for answers, arguments, or defenses in the Bible. These daily Scripture readings and prayers challenged me to stop seeking epiphanies and to immerse myself into something slow and steady—something in which growth is incremental and perhaps even imperceptible. (The anxious evangelical in me is still working on accepting that last one.) With the divine hours, the Bible became a different kind of devotional and spiritual tool than I had ever used before. Praying the hours daily is a way to be present with God and to sometimes hear God speak. I had stopped having "devotions" while in seminary because they felt like dead ends. But reading the Bible devotionally with the divine hours? It offered a promising way forward.

When I found Phyllis Tickle's *Divine Hours* and her devotional approach to praying with Scripture, I subverted my tendency to strain at Bible study in hopes of creating a spiritual experience. For most of my years as an evangelical, knowing the Bible and defending the faith had taken precedent over being present for God during prayer. Phyllis Tickle encouraged me to abandon that mindset and to instead primarily approach the Bible with a desire for God on God's own terms. Full stop. This proved a critical step toward contemplative prayer.

Epiphanies we might have while reading the Bible look different from this perspective as well. If I land on a deeper understanding of a Scripture passage's meaning, that's all well and good. But reading the Bible is not a game of spiritual hide-and-seek with a hard-to-get God. Thomas Merton writes, "The only thing to seek in contemplative prayer is God; and we seek Him successfully when we realize that we cannot find Him unless He shows Himself to us, and yet at the same time that He would not have inspired us to seek Him unless we had already found Him."[2] Reading and meditating on Scripture offer ways to rest in the presence of the God who has already found us. Proving the Bible and proving my own spiritual vitality had to stop being my primary tasks when reading Scripture. Rather, the Spirit has given us the Scriptures for the purpose of holy encounters and transformation.

I find it ironic now that I had used the word *devotions* for my time of Bible study before I started to actually read the Bible devotionally. There may be no better tool for this kind of devotional reading of Scripture than the divine hours.

The warmth and joy of Phyllis Tickle during our class conference call cut through the suspicion and anger I had long directed toward Catholicism. If she could find a place for this approach to prayer with deep Catholic roots, I reasoned that it wouldn't hurt me to give it a shot. After all, most of the prayers were based on Scripture. If I found a prayer that didn't fit my theological sensibilities, I could just skip it. It's not like the gatekeepers of evangelicalism needed to know that I was reading Scripture and praying daily from a prayer book derived primarily from Catholic prayer practices.

Thus I began covertly turning to Catholic prayers and prayer practices while remaining a committed Protestant. In a matter of ten years, my spiritual life had taken a rather unlikely turn: backward.

CAN READING THE BIBLE LESS HELP US MORE?

My specialty as a Protestant had long been Paul's epistles. Protestants really love Paul. You can't do anything more Protestant than lead a Bible study on Romans. If you participate in a small group that's been meeting for more than a few months and you haven't yet studied the book of Romans, there's probably a hotline you should call.

For years my devotions had been structured around reading a chapter of the Bible each day—sometimes two, if the chapters were short. I didn't want Jesus to think I was taking it easy. So the short bursts of Scripture in *The Divine Hours* can seem jarringly brief for Protestants. One commenter on a blogpost I wrote as I began meditating on shorter passages of Scripture (one or two verses at a time) shared a common objection: "Why would I settle for a snack when I can have a feast?!?!" Can you detect the mix of judgment and anxiety in that question? It's not just suggesting that I'm depriving myself spiritually and am in danger of starving my weak little soul; it's also suggesting that I'm lazy, or stupid, or both.

Of course I still read longer passages of the Bible. I have always attended churches that encourage this. And I have no problem with someone choosing a different approach to Scripture. But evangelicals can take a kind of firehose approach to the Bible, focusing on the quantity of verses read in each sitting rather than taking quality time to ponder a verse. It's as if there's some kind of potential or achievement we can unlock by reading more and more Scripture. While God can work with us however we practice, there is much to be gained by a slower, limited, and more reflective approach to Scripture.

We can actually gain more from Scripture if we read less of it. That isn't an absolute statement for all time, but it carries more than a measure of truth. Most evangelicals like me would throw an NIV Study Bible at anyone making such a preposterous statement. We love the Bible, and we're not going to let anyone love it more than we do or tell us that we should read it less—even if there are spiritual practices that go back centuries, even before Billy Graham, and have a long-standing track record of effectiveness.

LECTIO DIVINA

The church has used different approaches to Scripture over the years, but the practice of *lectio divina*, Latin for "divine reading," has proven especially enduring. In *lectio divina*, you choose a relatively short passage of Scripture and read it very slowly four times either alone or with a group. Each time you read the passage, you pay attention to different aspects of the passage. James Martin describes each step as a question to ponder while reading: "What does the text say? What is God saying to me through the text? What do I want to say to God about the text? What difference will the text make in my life?"[3] I frequently use one of the psalms from the morning prayer in the divine hours for a slower, more reflective time using these *lectio divina* questions.

In *Experiencing the Depths of Jesus Christ*, Jeanne Guyon describes a practice similar to *lectio divina*. Her version may be more palatable to evangelicals who are hungry for a "meal" of Scripture. She suggests reading a longer passage of Scripture and then focusing on a single verse for reflection and prayer. There isn't one right way to do this. The important thing is to approach Scripture with an awareness of God's presence and an open mind to the ways that God may direct you. People use different words to describe the ways that parts of the passage stand out to them. Some speak of this more cerebrally, while others say that a word or phrase may "shimmer" as they read it. I try to avoid overthinking this. In essence, if you notice something while slowly reading a verse or a few verses of Scripture, pause. Spend some time working through the four questions Martin names:

> What does the text say?
> What is God saying to me through the text?
> What do I want to say to God about the text?
> What difference will the text make in my life?

Lectio divina is not a path to a life-changing epiphany every time you read the Bible. To suggest as much would take us back down the road to evangelical anxiety. Rather, the goal is to rest in God's presence and to let the Spirit and Scripture do their work, even if that work may appear unspectacular or beyond our awareness. We remain open to the ways that God can speak to us. Spiritually speaking, our "work" in praying with Scripture is to abide. Abiding may be the restful waiting of contemplative prayer or the more mentally active meditations on Scripture. Once we are at rest and aware of God, we will be open for God to move. As an anxious evangelical, I had never realized that I'm not the one who knows what I need from God. God alone knows what I need. Why wouldn't I rest and trust that God will move in the ways I need when I set aside time for prayer?

Learning to pray isn't about epiphanies occurring or God poking us with reminders of his presence, although both certainly can happen. Prayer is an act of abiding that could take the active form of meditation on Scripture or the prayers of others, the restful practices of contemplative prayer, or my own praises and petitions. Regardless of how active I am, God produces fruits of love, peace, joy, and gentleness in his own time and in his own ways. Even the more spectacular prayers for healing or deliverance have a foundation of listening and awareness of God that is grounded in a sense of security in the Father's love as revealed by Jesus.

We have nothing to prove, to defend, or to fight for when we pray with the Scriptures. We are only devoting ourselves to God. We aren't in charge of producing results. We can train ourselves to be present and use practices such as reading the Bible devotionally to open ourselves to a present God.

Even today, while reading the divine hours from Tickle's book, the following psalm jumped out at me: "Teach me your way, O Lord, and I will walk in your truth; knit my heart to you that I may fear your Name" (Psalm 86:11). The two things that stood out to me are the actions that the psalmist asks God to take: "teach" and "knit." I have worked very hard to teach myself God's ways and to knit myself to God. How often have I struggled with fear and anxiety about not doing enough, learning enough, evangelizing enough, or being committed enough? Reflecting on this passage points me toward a greater sense of trust and dependence on God. It is God who teaches us his ways and knits us to himself. It's especially striking for me, a Bible-loving evangelical, to tell God, "Teach me your ways," when I have invested so much time in Bible study. These are the ideas that I can carry through my day. They bring peace and rest instead of prompting me toward fast-tracked spirituality or meeting some kind of standard or goal.

Reading the Bible devotionally takes our eyes away from concepts such as progress and personal spiritual growth. We are taking Jesus at his word and abiding in him, using Scripture to keep our minds focused on him. The shift in perception here may seem slight, but it's essential. We don't read the Bible to know the Bible or to improve ourselves spiritually. We read the Bible to be present with God. As we find peace and direction in the words of Scripture, we will be less distracted by marrying the cause of Christ to culture wars, elections, heresy hunts, theology debates, or religious measuring sticks. Devotional reading of the Bible using the divine hours and *lectio divina* can save us from making mistakes such as the following: "You search the scriptures because you think that in them you have eternal life; and it is they that testify on my behalf" (John 5:39).

I suspect that I will continue to evolve in my Bible reading practices and my understanding of how God speaks to us through Scripture. Yet I can rest easy, knowing that reading Scripture devotionally using a practice like *lectio divina* isn't some trend like fashion, exercise, or diet fads. Praying the hours with the global and historic church isn't a cultural trend that caters to the whims of a generation. This isn't a practice for slackers who want to get out of reading the Bible. If anything, praying the hours three or four times a day will help you read more Scripture at a sustainable pace and offer you time for focused reflection. You may find passages from Scripture that speak to your daily concerns as you go about your work, spend time with family, or run from one task to another.

PRACTICE THE PRACTICE

Pause for a moment to pray through one or two psalms. Set a timer for five, ten, or twenty minutes if that will help you focus. Choose your own psalm, or read through one of the verses below slowly.

On your first time through, pay attention to what it says.

The second time through, pay attention to what God may be speaking to you.

The third time, reflect on how you want to respond.

Finally, contemplate a word or phrase that could influence your life today.

The Lord is merciful and gracious, slow to anger and abounding in steadfast love. (Psalm 103:8)

O God, you know my folly; the wrongs I have done are not hidden from you. (Psalm 69:5)

FOUR

Cheat at Prayer

Recovering the Ancient Prayers of the Church

When you are praying, do not heap up empty phrases as the Gentiles do; for they think that they will be heard because of their many words.

—MATTHEW 6:7

A **S AN ANXIOUS EVANGELICAL**, I often worried about "praying wrong." I was especially worried about turning prayer into a sin. What could be worse than seeking a prayerful connection with God in one moment and the next moment transgressing the law of God? In my rebellion against Catholicism, I especially took to heart Jesus' command to avoid praying like the pagans, who believed their gods heard them because of their many words (Matthew 6:7). Christians who try to read the Bible literally, especially evangelicals, do not want to be like pagans. And the Catholic approach to prayer I had learned as a child sure felt like the empty pagan prayer practices against which Jesus warned.

In addition to recommending the repetition of the rosary, priests typically assign prayers for penance. A confession of being angry or lying may be met with a penance that involves reciting a series of prayers, such as ten Hail Marys and two Our Fathers. I would sulk out of the confession booth, kneel in a pew, and fly through the prayers as fast as my lips could move. Trying to squeak by with the bare minimum required of me, my approach was a far cry from contemplative prayer and from the sincere use of prayers passed down in the historic church.

Anyone can misuse a spiritual practice by going through the motions. Many Christians in many traditions have mistakenly tried to win favor from God. In fact, the Bible itself can be misused: read rapidly in order to hit a certain devotional goal, quoted out of context, or wielded as a weapon. But I don't see any Protestants, including evangelical ones, packing away their Bibles for the thrift store simply because the Bible can be misused. Similarly, any possible misuse should not prevent us from discovering the richness of ancient prayers in the loving pursuit of God.

When Jesus addressed the prayer practices of the pagans, note that he mentioned the assumption at the root of their prayers: that "they will be heard because of their many words." In other words, the longer you can stick it out and pray, the more likely a prayer will be heard. As a Catholic, I certainly made the mistake of praying like this—reciting prayers as a way to gain God's favor. But that isn't the final word on how these prayers, many of which are based on Scripture, can or should be used.

In fact, many Protestant churches have taken this to the opposite extreme, coming up with our own "freestyle" prayers. Some of us talk on and on, assuming God will be pleased by our many words. In my early days as an evangelical, I wanted to avoid useless repetition, and I unfortunately believed that I could come up with better spontaneous prayers than Jesus, the inspired writers of the Psalms, or the spiritual leaders of the historic church.

I have since learned that I can avoid making the mistake of the pagans, the halfhearted Catholics (as I used to be), and the anxious evangelicals by entering into prayer with the foundational truth that God loves us. Sometimes it may be more beneficial and edifying to recite a psalm or the Lord's Prayer (called "the Our Father" in the Catholic tradition) before praying in silence. These are the prayers that have been passed on to us from Jesus and his followers throughout the centuries. There's a reason why Christians around the world and throughout the history of the church have turned to these prayers. As we become aware of our limitations in belief and practice, the wider Christian family will benefit greatly from prayers that have been preserved in lectionaries, the Book of Common Prayer, and other prayer collections.

Prayer is the practice of becoming present for God's love. We cannot impress God with our many words or few words, our memorized prayers or our extemporaneous ones. We can no more win God's favor with the right turn of phrase than we can by reciting a favorite prayer one hundred times. If I ever end up trying to win God's favor by mindlessly repeating a prayer, I have not offended God so deeply that I must shelve that particular prayer or the Psalms forever.

Our fears of praying like the pagans are certainly rooted in a desire to make prayer meaningful and personal. But many of us have painted with such broad brushstrokes that we have missed out on a valuable church tradition. The prayer tradition of the church can help us become more present for God's transforming love.

TAKING PRAYER WITH US

My suspicion of Catholicism and its allegedly pagan prayer practices is best illustrated by my years-long resistance to praying the Our Father. The years of mindlessly repeating the Our Father for penance made it challenging to see any value in it as a devotional practice.

Like a good evangelical theology student, I dissected the prayer in order to derive principles for prayer and theological truth, and I stopped there. None of that helped me pray with greater clarity or frequency. But I sure had a bunch of notes with principles about prayer!

I finally turned back to praying the Our Father when I started swimming at a community pool a few days a week. A physical therapist examined my neck and shoulder pain issues, and her assessment was shockingly holistic. Beyond issues with my posture, my body was in a state of high alert and tension from my anxiety. She noted that my shoulders were arched up, as if I was bracing for a tiger attack. My response was, "Well . . . yeah." Doesn't everyone live in a constant state of fight or flight?

No, they don't, she assured me. As we discussed next steps, the therapist nudged me toward regular exercise. In hopes of finally getting my anxiety under control, alleviating the painful tension in my body, and being able to fall asleep at night, I joined the community center in our town. There I could swim, flail a bit on a stationary bike, or "run" around a track.

Anyone who starts an exercise routine from scratch knows what level of suffering this entails and that any distraction is more than welcome. Sure, I could occupy my mind with television or podcasts while running or riding a bike, but the pool became a problem. What should I think about in the pool so that I wouldn't obsess about the burning sensation in my legs?

I'd already been reading *The Divine Hours* for quite some time, and it made sense to take one of those prayers or Scriptures with me into the pool. Of course, taking one of those prayers with me into the pool would require actually memorizing it. At this point in my life, my laziness became a kind of grace from God. *The Divine Hours* includes the Our Father in every morning, noon, and vesper prayer time. As a self-righteous Protestant, I had taken the liberty of skipping it, lest I make the pagan repetition mistake. But I'd missed out on the simple fact that the Our Father is pulled directly from the words of Jesus. It's the way Jesus prayed. Yes, I had repeated it mindlessly for years as a form of penance. But did that make it worthless now? I reasoned that it couldn't hurt to live with the Our Father in my mind for twenty- to thirty-minute stretches while swimming in the pool a few days a week.

That year of living with the Our Father in my head for a sustained period helped me see why it has endured as an essential prayer for years. Far from exhausting this prayer that Jesus taught us to pray, I continue to be challenged by its simple statements. Am I approaching God as my Father? Am I trusting God to provide our daily bread? Are there people I am struggling to forgive? Am I depending on God's protection from temptation or evil?

We could do much worse than praying through these things daily. I didn't have any major epiphanies or life-changing moments. Rather, I sensed a gradual shift in my approach to prayer. I began to sense the sorts of things I could explore in prayer. Wealthy Christians in America could especially use more time meditating on what it looks like to ask God for our "daily" bread. Perhaps evangelicals repenting of their bids for political power or contributions to the culture wars can consider what it means for God's kingdom to come and God's will to be done on earth. Each day I am mindful that my own forgiveness before God is linked to the mercy I show to others. Besides the uncomfortable truth that it's hypocritical to ask God for mercy when I deny it to others, the experience of receiving God's forgiveness is a daily reminder of my own weaknesses that help me empathize with those I forgive. Relying on the prayers of the church has prompted me to pray in ways that I would have never considered on my own.

THE PRAYERS WE DON'T KNOW

Among the most humbling moments of my time praying with the divine hours has been reading the prayer of a Christian in China: "Help each of us, gracious God, to live in such magnanimity and restraint that the Head of the church may never have cause to say to any one of us, 'This is my body, broken by you.' Amen."[1]

As someone who deeply values the option of splitting off from religious groups that are either abusive or prone to theological error, the "protest" element of Protestant Christianity resonates with me. I like to think that I am the *Pro* in *Protestant*. It's embarrassingly easy to accuse, attack, and divide from Christians today. Even when someone is completely out of line, the possibilities for going overboard in my responses are endless.

Magnanimity and restraint? But did Jesus see what that person just tweeted? Didn't Jesus flip tables in his anger? By typing a mocking reply, I'm technically being quite restrained, right?

Stepping back from today's theology debates, controversies, and conflicts on social media, this prayer has forced me to consider my privilege as a Christian who has never faced persecution or serious conflict over my faith. From the comfort of the United States, where my faith is part of my country's fabric, I can afford to take shots at Christians who say ridiculous things. If a fundamentalist or dogmatic evangelical criticizes what I believe or the choices my family has made, I have nothing to lose if I turn my sarcasm loose. In a context where persecution is a real possibility, sarcasm is hardly a virtue.

Mind you, Christians suffering persecution will also be less likely to manufacture conflict or to create victim narratives by engaging in fruitless culture wars. Ecumenical cooperation has always been widely reported on the mission fields where there is significant adversity. So the question this prayer challenges me to ask is this: If Christians can figure out a way to get along when they're persecuted, why can't I sort out a way to live with magnanimity and restraint in a context of peace and religious freedom?

The prayers of the church have addressed far more than my sarcasm and zingers on social media. They have also challenged the prosperity that I took for granted, growing up in comfortable and safe neighborhoods. They have prompted me to be more poetic and imaginative in my prayers. They have shown just how limited my words are when praying.

For instance, take note of the words used in the following prayers. How do they engage with nature, prosperity, or pain, or with spirituality? Let these words settle into your mind and consider how they challenge or provoke you.

Disturb us, O Lord
> when we are too well-pleased with ourselves when our dreams have come true because we dreamed too little, because we sailed too close to the shore.

Disturb us, O Lord
> when with the abundance of things we possess, we have lost our thirst for the water of life

> when, having fallen in love with time, we have ceased to dream of eternity and in our efforts to build a new earth, we have allowed our vision of Heaven to grow dim.

Stir us, O Lord
> to dare more boldly, to venture into wider seas where storms show Thy mastery, where losing sight of land, we shall find the stars. In the name of Him who pushed back the horizons of our hopes and invited the brave to follow.[2]

O God, you have prepared in peace the path I must follow today. Help me to walk straight on that path. If I speak, remove lies from my lips. If I am hungry, take away from me all complaint. If I have plenty, destroy pride in me. May I go through the day calling on you, you, O Lord, who know no other Lord.[3]

Oh, my God, I want to love you
Not that I might gain eternal heaven
Nor escape eternal hell
But, Lord, to love you just because
you are my God.
Grant me to give to you
And not to count the cost,
To fight for you
And not to mind the wounds,
To labor and to ask for no reward except the knowledge that I
    serve my God.[4]

The diverse, rich experiences of the church can open us to new observations in our lives, to fresh perspectives on what we have, or to avenues of prayer that we simply don't know about thanks to our limited experiences. When I studied the theology of Latin American, Asian, and African scholars, I couldn't help noticing what stood out to them. The Tower of Babel was a story about the oppression of a powerful monoculture. The prodigal son is a story about immigration and hunger. The flight of Jesus to Egypt as a refugee certainly means something to a Latin American family fleeing violence. Perhaps if we opened ourselves to the ways God is working among the global and historic church, we will find deeper, more holistic ways to pray and to act.

THE PRAYERS WE AVOID

For years I had reasoned that I was smart and spiritual enough to figure out how to pray according to my own wisdom. But as I began praying the Our Father in the pool, I also found out why the church has treasured its prayer tradition. "Pray without ceasing," Paul tells his readers in 1 Thessalonians 5:17. Simply put, it's impossible to pray constantly by coming up with our own words. Returning to the Our Father felt a bit like putting the training wheels back on my bike. But as I humbled myself enough to begin learning from the traditions of the church, I saw that generations have long relied on praying with Scripture and the sturdy prayers of others. When I didn't know what to pray or even how to pray, I started to find strength in these prayers instead of seeing them as a sign of spiritual regression.

The prayers of the church also guide us into places we would otherwise avoid. We simply will never face the worst parts of ourselves and the best parts of God without a guide. Why did I even think that my own prayers were somehow superior to or more sincere than a prayer that came straight from Jesus? In my anxiety about being sincere, authentic, and strong enough to fashion my own prayers, I slipped into a self-sufficiency that veered close to pride. Now, as I embraced these prayers, I found that they offered words for prayer that I never would have considered using.

Sabbath. For example, each Saturday, the evening prayer in *The Divine Hours* concludes with a request for God to prepare our hearts for public worship on the following day.

Almighty God, who after the creation of the world rested from all your works and sanctified a day of rest for all your creatures: Grant that I, putting away all earthly anxieties, may be duly prepared for the service of public worship, and grant as well that my Sabbath upon earth may be a preparation for the eternal rest promised to your people in heaven; through Jesus Christ our Lord. Amen.[5]

This prayer has stopped me in my tracks often. How many Sundays have I crash-landed in church, having filled my week with work, worries, and entertainment? The prayer and worship of today can carry over into the way I worship and minister when gathered with others for public worship. Entering church with an awareness of God and my role within the church to hear God and pray for others is a dramatic switch from a consumer-focused approach to church.

Pausing. There's a sacred aspect to time and the cycle of each week. As we worship God at home, at our workplaces, or in the midst of our daily tasks, we create a rhythm for our days. We have prayers for the beginnings, transitions, and conclusions we face each day, reorienting ourselves around a kingdom mindset. Even the prayers that aren't based as directly on the time of day offer powerful words—words that may snap us out of our downward spirals of self-interest and personal indulgence so that we can pause to consider God's presence in our lives.

Grant that I, Lord, may not be anxious about earthly things, but love things heavenly; and even now, while I am placed among things that are passing away, hold fast to those that shall endure; through Jesus Christ our Lord, who lives and reigns with you and the Holy Spirit, one God, for ever and ever.[6]

Besides the more straightforward petitions of the liturgy of the hours or the Book of Common Prayer, we also find more poetic reflections, such as this prayer by John G. Whittier:

Drop thy still dews of quietness,
Till all our strivings cease;
Take from our souls the strain and stress,
And let our ordered lives confess
The beauty of thy peace.[7]

Suffering and death. Praying with the divine hours has also forced me to think and pray about suffering, sickness, and death. This evening prayer is a regular part of the compline at the end of each day:

Keep watch, dear Lord, with those who work, or watch, or weep this night, and give your angels charge over those who sleep. Tend the sick, Lord Christ; give rest to the weary, bless the dying, soothe the suffering, pity the afflicted, shield the joyous; and all for your love's sake. Amen.[8]

As a result of reciting this prayer each evening, I have incorporated a regular prayer for those who are homeless or living in threat of violence. I can no longer ask God for the safety of my own children while neglecting to pray for the safety of others, especially those living in the midst of immediate threats.

There is a general American trend of avoiding talk of suffering and death, and my sense is that many Christians have taken this trend of death avoidance to a whole other level. When there are so many entertaining distractions at our disposal in an affluent culture, we don't like to face either suffering or death. It's easier to focus on vision retreats, growth, and mission. Regular, sustained reflection on suffering and death simply isn't on our radar; many of us are preoccupied with preserving our own spiritual growth and the growth of our churches. Why would we face the darkness of death and the uncertainty of suffering when we can justify our affluence as God's blessing or busy ourselves with God's work? If we don't have any prayers to help us think otherwise, there's little chance that we'll prayerfully ponder suffering or death. It'll take experiencing a tragedy of our own to reorient our spirituality.

Surrender. Jesus told his followers that "today's trouble is enough for today" (Matthew 6:34), but it's all too easy to begin looking ahead to the cares and concerns of tomorrow. Rather than letting each day stand on its own, thanking God for his presence, and surrendering tomorrow to God's care, I have found it tempting to lie awake at night either lamenting my failures from the day or analyzing the challenges coming that week. The Final Thanksgiving from *The Divine Hours*, based on the prayer of Simeon, has snapped me out of my shame and restless worry. Simeon longed to see God's Messiah, and when he finally laid eyes on the child Jesus, he was content, letting loose his grip on whatever the future held. He relinquished himself to God's purpose. His words are integrated into this prayer that concludes each day:

> Lord, you now have set your servant free to go in peace as you have promised; for these eyes of mine have seen the Savior, whom you have prepared for all the world to see: a Light to enlighten the nations, and the glory of your people Israel. Glory to the Father, and to the Son, and to the Holy Spirit: as it was in the beginning, is now, and will be forever. Amen.[9]

Who doesn't need to be snapped out of personal plans and agendas for the future? These are the things on which we base our identities and our hopes. It's hard to imagine facing death with the peace and calm of Simeon, trusting that he had seen what God had intended him to see. I've been more of the kicking and screaming type, holding on for just one more day. I've spent time fearing what lies beyond and wishing for more time on earth. Praying Simeon's prayer each evening calls me away from the anxieties of our time and our collective fear of death. Simeon's words show me that we can depart in peace, faith, and hope. We have our course to run, and then we can only fall into the embrace of God.

LAUGHING WITH YOUR LAST BREATH

That hope of God's embrace is what prompted me to pursue contemplative prayer in the first place. Trusting that I can begin living in that loving embrace today is a powerful motivator. These prayers, rooted in the tradition of the church, can help us become aware of God's presence or can commission us to go out into the world as representatives of the gospel. Those who practice contemplation have often recited the Our Father, psalms, or other prayers from the church before or after silent prayer. These prayers can prepare us for the silence and stillness of contemplation.

For all my anxiety about facing the future, accomplishing meaningful things, and encountering death, I need to be repeatedly guided back to rest in prayer. There are treasures to uncover after meditating on the words of Simeon day in and day out. Those who have devoted themselves to prayer as Simeon did have found the hope of falling into God's embrace one day. There's a story of a monk living in the desert of Egypt who laughed while on his deathbed. The monks around him said, "'Tell us, Father, why you are laughing while we weep?' He said to them: 'I laughed the first time because you fear death. I laughed the second time because you are not ready for death. And the third time I laughed because from labors I go to my rest.'"[10]

I don't know if all of us can laugh as we draw our final breaths. But maybe contemplative prayer can move us away from the denial and fear of death in our consumerist society. The prayers of the church can give us the words we need to prepare us to wait on God in silence. They can snap us out of our restricted, tribal thinking and self-centered culture. They can draw us out of our anxiety that has big plans for next year but fears sickness and death. If the prayers of the church can help us find what we lack, the Examen is a daily practice that can reveal the true state of our souls as we begin to pray.

PRACTICING THE PRACTICE

Take a moment to sit with this prayer from *The Divine Hours*. Pray it slowly several times and pay attention to what stands out.

> Grant that I, Lord, may not be anxious about earthly things, but love things heavenly; and even now, while I am placed among things that are passing away, hold fast to those that shall endure; through Jesus Christ our Lord, who lives and reigns with you and the Holy Spirit, one God, for ever and ever.[11]

While I highly recommend investing in a hard copy of a prayer book like *The Divine Hours*, you can begin to experiment with praying the prayers of the church by visiting the Explore Faith website (ExploreFaith.org). You can enter in your time zone and pray the divine hours reading for that part of the day. The text is drawn directly from the edition compiled by Phyllis Tickle. Other apps and websites are available, but this version has been among the more user-friendly ones I have found.

FIVE

Don't Forget to Be Mindful

Practicing the Examen

When I trust deeply that today God is truly with me and holds me safe in a divine embrace, guiding every one of my steps, I can let go of my anxious need to know how tomorrow will look, or what will happen next month or next year. I can be fully where I am and pay attention to the many signs of God's love within me and around me.

—HENRI NOUWEN

AFTER THE BIRTH of our first child, I resolved to finally establish some kind of regular, scheduled prayer routine. I had always dived into prayer at random moments throughout my day, just talking with God about whatever came to mind. But once I was the primary caregiver for our child, my days followed the often unpredictable nap schedule of our son. Frantically trying to get work done whenever my wife could take care of our son, I found my time filled up. Prayer wasn't something that I could just turn to in the midst of my day.

I'd read about some parents soldiering on in their prayers through the middle of the night when a baby woke up crying. I'd heard of many other parents who saw their prayer lives more or less disappear. I feared that I would end up in the latter category if I didn't integrate something with a little more structure and intention into my life.

The great, yawning gap of time in those early days of parenting was the afternoon nap. I had heard parents speak of The Nap with reverence, as a critical period of the day. Now I understood. Everything pivots on The Nap. When The Nap goes smoothly, it bodes well for an afternoon of good fortune, with a refreshed child and parent who are able to push on through the waning hours of the day before The Bath, The Books, and The Bed. But when The Nap is a bad one or doesn't happen at all? Well, it's a screaming tragedy, leaving both child and parent in an endless void of exhaustion and emotional fragility that stretches for the rest of the day.

Our son did not nap.

The only way to coax him into a reliable nap was to take him for a walk. This plan worked well throughout the fall. In winter, I bundled him up in massive, puffy layers of down for walks all throughout Columbus, Ohio. A bike trail by our home offered thirty uninterrupted miles alongside a shallow river. A few tiny waterfalls along the way served as landmarks of a nap's success or struggle. Through rain, snow, or wind, I spent most afternoons walking my son in his jogging stroller along the path, hearing only an occasional chime of a bicycle bell, the chatter of workers from a nearby office taking a lunchtime walk, or the rustle of deer in the woods.

During these walks of an hour to an hour and a half, I had the option of playing podcasts or praying. I hoped to do the latter, and I had the best intentions. But once I was alone with my thoughts, I would spiral into a wreck of negativity, anger, fear, and anxiety. It was an insecurity parade: I worried about my work, our finances, and about anything and everything related to how people perceived me. It wasn't that I was struggling to pray. I was struggling to even get to the point where I could *attempt* to pray.

How do you pray when you can't even figure out how to start?

INTRODUCTION TO THE EXAMEN

This isn't a new problem, and thankfully, someone from the historic church spent a lot of time working through it. While recovering from a serious wound suffered in battle, Ignatius of Loyola began reading through Scripture and had a profound encounter with the risen Christ. As he pursued God in silence and meditation, he felt directed to develop a method of clarifying his thoughts before prayer. This practice, called the Examen, was a part of the spiritual exercises that he passed on to those in his community, which later became known as the Jesuits, or Society of Jesus.

The Examen is a series of prompts for reflection, a method of cultivating a greater awareness of God throughout the day. Ignatius instructed the Jesuits to practice the Examen twice daily, keeping track of their thoughts, emotions, and awareness of God so that they could pray with greater intention and focus.

There are different Examen methods and questions based on the spiritual practices of Ignatius. The basic structure of the Examen is as follows:

1. Become aware of God's presence.
2. Review the day with gratitude.
3. Pay attention to your emotions.
4. Choose one feature of the day and pray from it.
5. Look toward tomorrow.

I have found great benefit in the ways that the Examen cultivates awareness of my thoughts and emotions, increases my awareness of God, and helps me bring my daily thoughts and actions to God in prayer. Sometimes I focus on a particular question or aspect of the Examen. Other times the Examen reveals a deficit in my awareness of God. Most importantly, I have had to stop seeing the Examen as a kind of test of my spiritual progress. Despite its resemblance to the word *exam*, the

Examen is not an evaluation but rather a reset point in my day. It offers an opportunity to move forward with greater awareness of God and personal intention.

Methodists and students of church history may also recognize these prompts as similar to John Wesley's questions for self-examination. The main difference is that Wesley's questions are far more specific, while the Examen is open-ended and geared toward uncovering whatever is on your mind.

There's also a strong family resemblance between the Examen and the mindfulness practices advocated by psychology experts today. Many studies are finding that a few minutes of mindfulness make significant differences in the lives of both teachers and schoolchildren. In some contexts, time in a meditation room has replaced traditional punishments for children who act out, as teachers have realized that misbehaving is often linked with a child struggling to process stimuli.

Mindfulness helps us sift through our thoughts and emotions so that we can see the present moment with clarity. It can shut down ongoing loops of negative thinking, internal commentary, and mounting stress and anxiety. Mindfulness helps us restore a measure of power over our thoughts instead of being at their mercy. Ignatius recognized the value of this hundreds of years ago as he developed the Examen practice with its valuable prompts that help practitioners gauge their awareness of God throughout the day.

I first attempted contemplative prayer before I learned about the Examen, and I was a hot mess. Nothing made sense or worked when I sought silence before God. I felt lost and completely at the mercy of my thoughts, which ranged all over the place. Without the personal assessment of the Examen, any hope of rest or surrender to God remained disrupted or redirected when I sat down to pray. In my bid for silence and prayer, I was facing the truth about myself and my thoughts. As Richard Rohr writes, "Before the truth sets you free, it tends to make you miserable."[1]

Early on in my contemplative journey, I made the mistake of approaching prayer as a kind of dumping ground for my thoughts. But I've found that it's actually better to dump out my thoughts *before* I pray, and to do so by practicing the Examen. That frees my mind to be present for God. Doing the Examen before I pray offers clarity about which thoughts need to be explored further in prayer. Contemplative prayer is much like a plant: it only puts down roots after we have tilled the hard soil of our anxious minds with a practice like the Examen.

Getting our thoughts sorted out with a daily Examen practice removes the pressure from our prayer time. We don't have to make ourselves think particularly holy thoughts or create some kind of experience. Thomas Merton writes, "The reason why so many religious people believe they cannot meditate is that they think meditation consists in having religious emotions, thoughts, or affections of which one is, oneself, acutely aware."[2] This focus on giving thoughts and emotions free rein during prayer can also result in heightened expectations for some kind of resolution to come about during prayer. Merton continues, "As soon as they start to meditate, they begin to look into the psychological conscience to find out if they are experiencing anything worthwhile. They find little or nothing. They either strain themselves to produce some interior experience, or else they give up in disgust."[3] The Examen frees us to work through a time of self-reflection separate from our moments of silent prayer. We can ask where God has been in our lives, become aware of the thoughts in our minds, surrender our thoughts to God, and invite God into each area of our lives. The pressure is off when we begin to pray, and we need only become available to God.

DOES THE EXAMEN ACTUALLY COUNT?

Lest you think I'm more spiritually accomplished than I actually am, the main reason I persevered in practicing the Examen— even after my son started napping in his bed regularly—was a simple iPhone app. While there are several Examen apps, the one I found is called Examine, and it offers the perfect opportunity to use my iPhone for a noble purpose. The Examine app has a timer that concludes the period of silence with a little chime. How I loved to hear that chime!

Practicing the Examen for three months completely exposed overlooked areas of my spiritual practices and nudged me toward positive steps forward. As I reflected on the positive and negative elements of each day, I started to notice a troubling pattern: most of my positive moments were tied to my work. I clearly relied too much on my work as a barometer for each day. Consequently, I also worried quite a bit about money—how to make it, why I couldn't save it, and when I had to spend it. Many of my struggles over providing for my family and trusting God came into sharper focus once I developed a regular practice to reflect on each day.

Ironically, anxious evangelicals like me sometimes struggle to see the value of the Examen because we think the practice will keep us trapped inside our own heads. We wonder, How can reflecting on my day possibly have any spiritual value?

I'll be the first to admit that practicing the Examen didn't actually feel "spiritual." I was just thinking about my day, after all. This is typically not the way that anxious Christians who are trying to prove themselves pursue God! When you've thought of prayer as talking to God and believed you can only grow spiritually by working harder at it and doing it better, it's difficult to believe that mindfulness through the Examen really counts as a spiritual practice. Aren't there more important spiritual matters to which we should give ourselves?

For Saint Ignatius, however, the Examen was a nonnegotiable. He taught that if you can only find time for one spiritual practice, this is it. It's as if Saint Ignatius knew that any struggle to find time or focus for prayer could be resolved if you remain prayerfully aware of yourself through the Examen. The Examen offers what I've needed the most: an invitation to step outside my own head so that I can see where my mind is going and how aware I am of God.

In addition to helping us take stock of our thoughts and emotions, the Examen can also help us take stock of our bodies and how our emotions are manifesting themselves physically. Anxious energy, whether from evangelical Christianity or from my own personal issues, can show up in the ways I hold my body, clench my fists, squeeze my feet in tense positions, breathe uneasily, or arch my shoulders. As I learned to become aware of my thoughts, I started to notice the ways my body had been offering clues to my mindset. My body offered its own kind of Examen about the state of my thinking, indicating whether I was resting in God or fearful of a situation.

All this talk of mindfulness and body awareness may sound to some Christians like a slippery slope away from Christianity. But the magic of a slippery slope is in its completely unverifiable nature. Taking an alleged "slippery slope" seriously appears to be wise and cautious. Even the appearance of slipping is to be avoided if you take your faith seriously, right? But some slippery slopes are just a fabrication of Christian paranoia. Slippery slope thinking thrives on the questions, Who knows what could happen next? Why risk it?

The particularly conservative Christian suspicion of spiritual practices may be rooted in the fear of slippery slopes toward Catholicism or Eastern religions. The Examen appears to send us sliding in both directions—with the added "danger" that such mindfulness may call to mind secular mindfulness practices. For anxious Christians, there is no telling what will happen once you're on a yoga mat practicing mindfulness (although I'm pretty sure the most likely outcome is a post-yoga trip to Starbucks, not losing your faith).

TAKING UNHEALTHY THOUGHTS CAPTIVE

The Examen offers a hopeful starting point for prayer. It discloses not only that we have a measure of control over our thoughts but that God is with us in the present and is able to help us stop obsessing over the past and the future. Thomas Merton assures us that this is an essential step in prayer. He writes, "One cannot then enter into meditation, in this sense, without a kind of inner upheaval. By upheaval I do not mean a disturbance, but a breaking out of routine, a liberation of the heart from the cares and preoccupations of one's daily business."[4] There is no summoning of God or convincing God to take pity on us as we struggle with our fears and anxiety. God doesn't play cat-and-mouse games with us, withholding his presence if we don't say the right words.

Jesus said, "Come to me, all you that are weary and are carrying heavy burdens, and I will give you rest" (Matthew 11:28). I have found that the Examen is a way to bring my worries and anxious thoughts to God, exposing these dark clouds to God's penetrating light. In addition to gaining clarity in my thoughts, I can invite God to take my unhealthy thoughts captive.

Richard Rohr reminds us that our healing comes through our sins and failures. Our sins and failures typically reveal our deepest wounds and needs—both of which need God's presence of healing and restoration. "You cannot heal what you do not first acknowledge," writes Rohr in *Breathing Under Water.*[5] He takes it a step further: "In terms of soul work, *we dare not get rid of the pain before we have learned what it has to teach us.*"[6]

What makes Jesus so unbelievable to many of us is that he calls us to become more honest than we are able to be on our own. Only he knows the depths of my fears, the ways I truly lean on my own resources and plans, and the ways that I have made him unnecessary in my life. In many cases, my sins, fears, and anxieties are the products of trying to make it through life on my own. Typically, my sins are the ways I try to cope and manage with life, while my anxieties are often rooted in my reaction to circumstances that appear threatening or beyond my control. The Examen breaks through my illusions, helping me to see each day just how far I have drifted from Christ. It illuminates all the ways I deal with life on my own. As I face these broken parts of myself, I am in a position where I can pray honestly.

Each time I pause to become aware of God, face my thoughts, and look for the ways that God has been at work in my day, I open myself to God's power and presence. My friend Preston Yancey writes in his book *Out of the House of Bread* that the Examen is especially useful for seeing what has gone well. Many days I have been so focused on all that I haven't done, couldn't do, or have done wrong. On those days, the Examen prompts me to focus on the positive aspects of my day and to find God present in these as well. I have become far more thankful since I started practicing the Examen. Thankfulness is an essential part of spirituality, as the Psalms tell us to enter God's presence with thanksgiving.

The act of confronting my thoughts directly gave me greater control over them so that I could offer my thoughts to God. If we're all busy, distracted people who struggle to focus while praying, then we need to stop running from our thoughts. Until we face our distractions, see them for what they truly are, and bring them under God's rule, we'll continue to wonder why it's so hard to focus while attempting to pray.

DIGITAL DISTRACTION, ANXIETY, AND THE EXAMEN

Personal restoration and prayer are hard to fit into our schedules, and they're even harder to protect. Before I had regular, meaningful time for reflection, I didn't know what it felt like to be at rest in God, let alone to be aware of my internal monologue. I can't tell you how many times I've passed up a moment for quiet reflection in favor of something else. I can always find a reason to keep pushing forward on a work project, to tackle a household chore, reply to a text or email, or settle for whatever entertainment I can dig up on my computer in the evening—especially during hockey season.

The more that technology is at my fingertips—from smartphones to tablets to any number of other devices—the greater the temptation to keep checking in, to keep conversations going, or to seek a bit of distraction. I have started to keep my phone with me at all times, experiencing a mild panic on the occasions that I leave it at home. That emotion alone is well worth exploring!

Ironically, this kind of digital connection frequently leads to both relational and spiritual disconnections if left unchallenged and unexamined. I used to drive eleven hours to college without a cell phone. If I had a flat tire, I had to unload the trunk, roll out the spare, and figure out where to stick the jack. I can only presume that if my car had broken down, I would have just died somewhere along the side of the road. It's also incredible that my wife and I remained married for so long without our own cell phones. We were really living dangerously each time I went to the supermarket without a cell phone, unable to contact her if the store was out of the flour she put on the list or if she forgot to mention how many potatoes I should pick up. The stakes feel ridiculously high with the level of connection we take for granted with our phones, tablets, and computers.

The Examen has been an essential part of my recovery from digital distraction and my captivity to intrusive technology. I now understand the ways that I use these tools to avoid facing my fears and anxieties. I have found that technology tends to encourage "mindlessness." The mindlessness of digital devices is a far greater threat to Christian spirituality than any mindfulness practice alleged to resemble an Eastern religious practice.

In fact, without the focused mindfulness of practices such as the Examen, we'll have every incentive to run from our fears, pain, and faults. Who wants to dwell on the complexities and fears of the present when escape is just a tap away?

While anxious Christians may fear that the Examen is little more than a self-centered exercise for spiritual slackers, it has saved me from unwitting compromise with the ways of this world, from distraction, and from anxiety and fear. If I was ever on a slippery slope away from God, it was before the Examen revealed just how far my anxieties, fears, and entertaining distractions had pulled me away from God's presence.

With the Examen turning over the rock-hard soil of my mind so that prayer could finally take root, I was able to learn what the psalmist meant when he wrote, "For God alone my soul waits in silence, for my hope is from him" (Psalm 62:5). Having learned to stop relying on my own words for prayer and to turn over my anxious thoughts, I was finally ready to learn what it meant to flee into solitude so that I could be present for God.

PRACTICING THE PRACTICE

Incorporating all five Examen questions each day may be a challenge for some. While apps like the Examine (as of this writing, available only for iPhone) or Reimagining the Examen provide a helpful guide that many find beneficial, it may be more helpful to begin with two simple practices.

Step 1: Pay attention. Take notice of the blessings around you each day and express gratitude. Notice how you are feeling in stressful situations, and identify your emotions and responses. Take advantage of a time to rest. Take a moment to be playful or creative. Be aware of how you react to exhaustion. This isn't a test or an evaluation.

Step 2: Ask, "Where is God?" As an anxious evangelical struggling with doubts about God, I did not love this question. However, if you can trust that there is a loving God who is present right now for you, this can become a restful practice throughout your day. God is present in the sunrise that colors over a gray morning sky. God is present in the joy of a child at play. God is present in your sadness and disappointment. God is present when you sit down to rest or rise to leave for work. This is simply an extension of paying attention in step 1. God is present in your day. The next step is to notice where God is working in your life.

SIX

Retreat

Making Peace with Solitude

The solitary life, being silent, clears away the smoke-screen of words that man has laid down between his mind and things.

—THOMAS MERTON

I N THE VALLEY of Vermont you can't miss the massive lump of Mount Equinox, which emerges from an otherwise standard ridgeline. Equinox once had a hotel at the summit, where guests could enjoy fierce storms, high winds, and views of the town of Manchester, Vermont, part charming vacation village and part run-of-the-mill suburban outlet shopping center. Manchester and its surrounding landscape of ridgelines and modest mountains offer sanctuary for both rugged outdoor adventurers and the extravagantly wealthy.

Tucked away on the west side of Mount Equinox away from the bustling village of Manchester, there's an entirely different sort of village. Hiding on the mountain's steep slopes is a Carthusian monastery.

I used to think about the monks every time my wife and I set out on a day hike of Equinox. As I trudged around the summit, seeking out the more solitary lookout spots that were sheltered from tourists who had driven up the access road, I kept thinking about those monks, who rarely talk or leave the monastery grounds.

Those monks sure were missing out! I mean, just over the mountain the monks could find fine restaurants run by award-winning chefs, art galleries, bakeries, one of the best independent bookstores in America, and plenty of concerts and cultural events. Although travel writer Bill Bryson derides the parasitic outlets of Manchester in one spare sentence in his book *A Walk in the Woods*, Manchester still offered the perks of a cozy little village nestled in the mountains—if you knew where to go. Those monks on Mount Equinox seemed to take a rejection of commercialism to the extreme.

But the more I joked about those monks who were missing out, the more uneasy I became. Maybe monks make some people uneasy because they're so quiet. I mean, what are those guys *really* thinking about? As a young married man, I could not identify with their experience. In addition, I couldn't imagine venturing off into the woods for the rest of my life, let alone taking a vow of silence in the solitude of a lonely building.

Today, with three little kids bouncing off the furniture, I'll admit that a little solitude sounds great—for an hour or ten. Yet I still find it hard to imagine what could drive those monks to run off into great silence. Why would they choose silence and solitude as a way of life? How could they flee the fullness of a life of conversation and activity? And is there something for anxious Christians to learn from them in terms of truly craving solitude and silence before God? I can assure you that evangelicals like me have spent more time thinking about worship music sets or new ways to study the book of Romans than pondering the solitude of a few monks living on the side of a mountain.

As I began my contemplative journey, I struggled mightily until I made my peace with solitude and the silence that comes with it.

WHY RETREAT?

What is the most American evangelical thing an American evangelical can do? One word: *advance*. In fact, Advance was the name of an event a ministry affiliated with my former church proclaimed that it would host. This wasn't a *retreat*. Retreats are going the wrong direction, folks! The people leading the Advance surely meant well, and I'm sure some good came of it. Yet once you ponder the implications of replacing the word *retreat* with the word *advance*, you find an encapsulation of the mindset that drives anxious Christian spirituality, especially American evangelicals. We must always move forward. We must always make progress—even if moving "backward" or stopping could be really good for our mental, physical, and spiritual health. A retreat? That's just admitting weakness, or a lack of determination and commitment. Did Jesus retreat when he carried the cross? No! He advanced, and so should you!

My own camp of American evangelicals tends to ask questions like, If you've fought and clawed and worried about your spiritual progress, why would you retreat and risk losing momentum? Why would you retreat when the real solution is to advance and to claim victory? Besides, victors don't conquer the enemy by retreating. Evangelicals sometimes gravitate toward the spiritual warfare language of the Bible at the expense of the language that describes waiting or resting in God.

Most anxious Christians aren't quite bold enough to literally replace a retreat with an advance; they simply pack their "retreats" with lots of activities. When I finally took a retreat years after I'd begun my contemplative journey—at an actual retreat center—I kept wondering what to do with myself. How would I keep myself busy, without having my day scheduled down to the minute? Praying for an hour suddenly seemed like an eternity, and a jam-packed "advance" schedule started looking a lot better. I tried to retreat, but in my heart, I really wanted to advance.

Growing up evangelical, I had plenty of reasons to dismiss solitude before I had even experienced it. Perhaps my greatest barrier to solitude came from a movement that simply didn't value fleeing the concerns and challenges of each day. It's not easy to shift from a busy, frantic, anxious spirituality into the stillness of silence or the unscheduled nature of solitude.

When I attempted a silent retreat while in seminary, I carried my anxiety with me, worrying that I was doing silence "wrong" and not getting enough benefits from my focused time with God. I read the Bible, talked to God a bit, and wandered around the woods for six hours. Nothing much came of it, and my mind kept wandering back to the diner a few miles from the trailhead. They probably had all-day breakfast—and pie!

Like a typical anxious evangelical, I even turned the solitude of a retreat into an evaluation or demonstration of my spirituality. I wanted some confirmation from God that I was on the right track. I wanted verification and personal justification. Sure, I was "retreating" by outward appearance, but I still wanted to advance.

While I'll never enter into a life of silence and solitude like those Carthusian monks up on Mount Equinox, I finally admitted that perhaps I was the one missing out on something really important.

THE URGENCY OF SOLITUDE

My tipping point toward a contemplative spirituality occurred when I read yet another book in seminary that argued that our struggles with sin and negative thinking all boiled down to wrong information. Wrong living could easily be repaired by right thinking, the author asserted. Sin resulted from not knowing enough truth or not committing to the truth.

But I'd been pumping my brain full of the "right" theological information for more than ten years, and I didn't appear to be any closer to God or to any kind of transformation. If anything, I was beginning to lose hope that I would ever draw any closer to God. I knew the Scripture verse that said, "Return to me . . . and I will return to you" (Zechariah 1:3). But was "returning" to God simply a matter of intellectual affirmation? My experiences in Christianity at that point suggested that my knowledge had very little to do with actual spiritual formation. I was saturated with words and ideas about God, but I longed for the presence of God.

I know I wasn't alone. So many friends, family members, and colleagues hit a similar wall. Many of my seminary friends would be the first to tell you about the limits of stockpiling biblical and theological knowledge for life transformation.

Catholic author Henri Nouwen, who left teaching posts at Yale and Harvard to minister among those with intellectual disabilities, also grew weary of the many words of ministry. In *The Way of the Heart*, Nouwen assures us that the solitary spirituality of the early mothers and fathers of the desert can offer a time-tested relief from our many words. "Solitude is the place of the great struggle and the great encounter—the struggle against the compulsions of the false self, and the encounter with the loving God who offers himself as the substance of the new self."[1] Nouwen then cuts even more directly to the heart of the matter: "The wisdom of the desert is that the confrontation with our own frightening nothingness forces us to surrender ourselves totally and unconditionally to the Lord Jesus Christ."[2]

If Bible study and theology had helped me develop a sense of control over how I interacted with God, solitude became my great moment of surrender. Pursuing God in solitude was a leap of faith that put me entirely at God's mercy, without the security of theological concepts or my own ideas. Instead of justifying myself before God as one who is grateful that he isn't a heretical sinner like so many others, I had to fall on my knees and confess the foolishness of my wisdom. I became a vine, clinging to the branch for dear life, because that's all a vine knows how to do. I could not theologically reason myself into a spiritual transformation that bore useful fruit for God's kingdom.

SOLITUDE IN REAL LIFE?

The typical parent of small children can hardly go to the bathroom in private, let alone maintain twenty minutes of silence and stillness. Save for the sweet repose of naps and bedtime, we who have small children have very little solitude—and even a child's naps and bedtime are the very moments when everything from cooking to cleaning to laundry to bills demands our attention.

Thomas Merton respected those with callings separate from his own. He also had compassion for the interruptions they faced and their lack of the daily support of a community, in which one has like-minded believers just down the hall.

Whether washing dishes, taking a walk, or just lying in bed at night, I have learned in my busiest seasons that spaces can still be preserved for a measure of solitude. Yet, the problem greater than *finding* solitude has been *valuing* solitude. The immediate benefits are not easy to quantify, and plenty of other urgent matters fill up my time. In fact, I rarely think solitude is something I need. If I don't value solitude, then I won't make the sacrifices necessary to find space for it.

When I think of the desert fathers and mothers taking to the wilderness to create space for God, my first thought is that they were punishing themselves rather than taking a positive step toward God. The idea of wandering in the wilderness or pursuing solitude has been framed in a mostly negative light in my own evangelical circles. The idea of wandering in the wilderness or seeking God in solitude is actually quite positive or at least necessary from the perspectives of many writers of Scripture. Beyond discovering why the Bible portrays solitude in a positive light, I have had to face the reasons behind my own resistance to it.

In the discipline of solitude, I had to relinquish control and wisdom before the greatness of God because I finally saw things as they truly are. Any attempt to engineer my own transformation broke down. Any resolve, resolution, or right thinking to do a better job of finding God eventually ended in failure or feeling inadequate.

Solitude isn't a cure-all. It's no guarantee for a vibrant spiritual life. But it has become a vital refuge that saves me, over and over again, from my own inadequate remedies and faulty illusions of myself and others. Henri Nouwen speaks of solitude as a "furnace of transformation": "Without solitude we remain victims of our society and continue to be entangled in the illusions of the false self."[3] Being freed from the illusions of the false self: I can think of no better thing for anxious Christians who have come to the limits of personal effort and knowledge. Entering solitude with open hands can free us to receive whatever God will give us. I have often gone into solitude with my own plans and agenda. Having dedicated so much time to theological study, I wasn't comfortable with mystery for quite some time, especially with a mysterious God. Solitude strips away the script that theology can provide for God. In silence before God alone, I am forced to surrender any Scripture verses that I might manipulate in my moment of need, as if I could trap God by using his own words against him. In the silence, I can only surrender to the mystery of God.

GIFTS OF SOLITUDE

There are deep mysteries to God's love and presence, and solitude is one of the ways I have inched closer to them. What I know of God's love and presence feels very much like drops of water from a limitless stream. What we've come to believe and trust may crumble to dust in the pursuit of solitude. This is just as well. Any illusions or false conceptions of ourselves or of God will crumble eventually. Solitude preemptively exposes our illusions before they let us down in the midst of a crisis. In solitude, we "die" to ourselves so that God can raise us up. Nouwen writes, "In solitude, our heart can slowly take off its many protective devices, and can grow so wide and deep that nothing human is strange to it."[4]

Brennan Manning saw solitude as an essential step toward truly seeing ourselves, others, and God:

Silent solitude makes true speech possible and personal. If I am not in touch with my own belovedness, then I cannot touch the sacredness of others. If I am estranged from myself, I am likewise a stranger to others. Experience has taught me that I connect best with others when I connect with the core of myself. When I allow God to liberate me from unhealthy dependence on people, I listen more attentively, love more unselfishly, and am more compassionate and playful. I take myself less seriously, become aware that the breath of the Father is on my face and that my countenance is bright with laughter in the midst of an adventure I thoroughly enjoy. Conscientiously "wasting" time with God enables me to speak and act from greater strength, to forgive rather than nurse the latest bruise to my wounded ego, to be capable of magnanimity during the petty moments of life.[5]

When Christianity became the official religion of the Roman Empire, the desert fathers and mothers saw solitude as a way to replace martyrdom. In his introduction to the spirituality of the desert fathers and mothers, John Chryssavgis writes, "The voice of the desert's heart replaced the voice of the martyr's blood. And the Desert Fathers and Mothers became witnesses of another way, another Kingdom."[6] There was no surer way than solitude to strip away what they depended on in place of God. (I address this in greater detail in chapter 9.) This was a kind of "death" for them, which led to new life. They sought the union with Christ that Paul spoke of in 1 Corinthians 6:17 and Romans 8:9-11, and they set aside every possible distraction. Nouwen assures us that "solitude molds self-righteous people into gentle, caring, forgiving persons who are so deeply convinced of their own great sinfulness and so fully aware of God's even greater mercy that their life itself becomes ministry."[7]

While anxious Christians may pay lip service to an indwelling Spirit or a kind of union with Christ that is possible for the saved, we aren't exactly sure how this indwelling or union happens. If anything, I spent years looking for some kind of confirmation or proof that I had the Spirit dwelling in me. I spent years working harder, studying more, and seeking earnestly. Only in solitude did I surrender to the great mystery of God that waited for me.

In hindsight, I can roll my eyes at my years of anxious spiritual searching and haphazard striving. I still get a kick out of the "advance" idea. The thing is, the benefits of solitude truly do appear to be counterintuitive. Thomas Merton wrote about the moment he walked into his monastery to stay: "Brother Matthew locked the gate behind me and I was enclosed in the four walls of my new freedom."[8] That notion still sends me into a bit of a panic. I like being able to travel, to drive wherever I want and whenever I want—within reason. How could someone find real freedom within the constraints of such limitations?

Solitude is an urgent need for Christians today as we struggle to find a space for walking with God while we are addicted to technology, as we cope with the urgent demands of each day, and as we wonder how to find a space for acting justly, let alone mercifully. The problems we face are easy to see, but the long-term impact of solitude is difficult to anticipate. Perhaps we have to take its promise on faith. Most importantly, anxious Christians who are preoccupied with visible benchmarks will struggle to see not only how solitude and silence could fit into their spiritual formation but how they can form a new foundation. Returning to the story of Abba Arsenius and finding our place in it may offer us a path forward.

WHY SOLITUDE MATTERS

Surely many of us relate to the request of Abba Arsenius, who prayed: "Lord, lead me in the way of salvation." He then heard a voice saying, "Arsenius, flee, be silent, pray always, for these are the sources of sinlessness." We all want to be led in the way of salvation. We all want to be sinless. The response from God, however, counters what many evangelicals like me have valued. While this message was given directly to Abba Arsenius in response to his request, there has been a consistent resemblance among contemplatives throughout the history of the church. In one way or another they have fled from some aspect of daily life, welcomed silence, and devoted themselves to a form of listening prayer.

Contemplatives who pursue silence and prayer—such as the desert fathers and mothers so long ago—reportedly radiated the love and peace of God. Their time in solitude turned them into people who could testify about God's loving presence by the ways they interacted with people. We know so much about the desert mothers and fathers and their experiences because so many people ventured into the desert to learn from them and to seek their advice. On one occasion, the following exchange occurred:

> Theophilus of holy memory, Bishop of Alexandria, journeyed to Scete, and the brethren coming together said to Abbot Pambo: Say a word or two to the Bishop, that his soul may be edified in this place. The elder replied: If he is not edified by my silence, there is no hope that he will be edified by my words.[9]

Perhaps we struggle to imagine anything edifying about sitting in someone's presence. But some of my most profound exchanges with deeply spiritual people have been rooted directly in their presence, not in their words. People committed to solitude communicate attention and love through their simple presence rather than merely their words. It was God's loving presence that prompted the desert fathers and mothers to flee into the desert, and those who visited them experienced their compassion and mercy. Saint Anthony ventured even deeper into the desert because his original cell was overrun by visitors.

The influence of the desert mothers and fathers was deeply grounded in a simple spirituality that had no use for publicity, controversy, or spectacles that drummed up crowds. Can you imagine packing up every American Christian, sending them off to the most remote places in the country, and then waiting for visitors to show up seeking advice? Merely joking about such a plan would elicit a chapter-and-verse response from many Christians: "Didn't Paul employ the 'biblical' approach to outreach that targets urban centers?" "Haven't you read about the great commission?"

WHAT ABOUT OUTREACH AND ACTIVISM?

Many Christians have shifted to a kind of extreme with our emphasis on outreach and public presence, even as we have let go of the vital place of solitude in our faith. I'm certainly not saying that every Christian leader should go out into the wilderness—although I wish a few of the more outspoken culture warriors would give it a whirl. I also don't want to lose sight of the fact that evangelicals and like-minded Christians have done a tremendous amount of good in the world—from giving humanitarian aid to providing medical care to helping those with addiction issues to caring for those without families and support networks. Yet in our zeal to gain influence in order to advance the gospel, our neglect of solitude has become painfully evident. Many Christians have become so afraid of not making progress that we haven't stopped to consider the very real possibility that our misguided actions could send the gospel into reverse at top speed.

It's a false dichotomy to suggest that solitude is the opposite of an engaged life. As isolated as the desert fathers and mothers may have been, their solitude actually became a ministry to the people of their day—to say nothing of the ways their writings have benefited future generations. Thomas Merton explains their mission like this: "They had come into the desert to be themselves, their ordinary selves, and to forget a world that divided them from themselves. There can be no other valid reason for seeking solitude or for leaving the world. And thus to leave the world, is, in fact, to help save it in saving oneself."[10] These desert fathers and mothers withdrew from the arguments and concerns of their day to serve others from a place of wholeness, peace, and connection with God. "They knew that they were helpless to do any good for others as long as they floundered about in the wreckage," Merton adds. "But once they got a foothold on solid ground, things were different. Then they had not only the power but even the obligation to pull the whole world to safety after them."[11]

Catholic spiritual writers today are very aware of this tension between solitude and activism. Richard Rohr is quick to note the ways that Franciscan friars aimed to correct the disconnection of the religious establishment, linking contemplation with action at his aptly named organization, the Center for Contemplation and Action. (I'll address the intersection of contemplation and activism more in chapter 10.) Thomas Merton lived as a particularly quiet Trappist monk, but he remained engaged in the issues of his time, including war, racial injustice, and politics, often putting himself at odds with brothers at his abbey and with Catholic leaders in the United States. Merton occasionally traveled to speak at conferences, and he never presented solitude as something reserved for monks or clergy. He wrote, "As soon as a man is fully disposed to be alone with God, he is alone with God no matter where he may be—in the country, the monastery, the woods or the city."[12] Far from cutting himself off from the world, Merton carried his solitude with him and shared its fruits in his writings. He ministered out of his solitude, and rather than scolding those who worked, parented, or carried out the many other tasks of daily life, Merton praised their far more limited solitude and contemplation since they faced many more obstacles than the average monk.

WILDERNESS TIMES

While the solitude of the wilderness could be a place of punishment and refining, many Christians see it in a mostly, if not wholly, negative light. Evangelicals often speak of our hardest times as a kind of wilderness. Whether that "wilderness" is a time of personal doubts or a season without a supportive church community, a retreat into the wilderness of solitude can present us with a singular opportunity to focus on God and God alone. Merton hails solitude as a kind of spiritual Eden, reframing the wilderness wanderings of Israel as a blessing rather than a punishment. "God's plan was that [the Israelites] should learn to love Him in the wilderness and that they should always look back upon the time in the desert as the idyllic time of their life with Him alone."[13] Yes, we could see the wilderness wandering of the people of Israel as a punishment from God. But isn't it more accurate to say that the Hebrew people needed that time to completely surrender their future to God? When we see how the history of Israel unfolded, it's not unreasonable to suggest that they could have used quite a few more journeys through the wilderness!

Of course it's not easy for me to leave my comfortable home, my busy schedule, and my "important" plans to venture into the wilderness of solitude. There's no telling what will happen, let alone if God will appear in any way. Will a retreat just be a waste of time that will set me back and only add to my daily stress? Or will it lead me deeper into an awareness of God's presence?

Pursuing solitude can certainly result in an advance, but the movement comes from God rather than from us. In other words, we cannot engineer our own spiritual advances. In solitude, we move our own agendas and wisdom out of the way so that God's kingdom can advance. Then, with the clarity afforded by solitude, we can join God.

If solitude helps us "advance" in any way, it is away from our false or incomplete notions about ourselves, others, and God. Perhaps the typical anxious evangelical like me struggles to see the wisdom of a retreat or a moment of solitude because there is so much that needs to be stripped away. We carry so much that we can't see, much less join, where God is taking us. Only when we surrender and retreat into solitude will we be able to join God in his kingdom's advance. When we truly experience solitude, we'll remove the distractions that surround us and prepare ourselves to become silent before God.

Rather than imagining all that I didn't want to give up if I were to join a secluded monastery on the side of a Vermont mountain, I could have imagined what I was missing. When I began to experience solitude firsthand, even if I typically spent only five or twenty or thirty minutes each day, I discovered that solitude with God was the spiritual practice I'd been craving since I began reading my Slimline NIV Bible in middle school and praying in earnest. The practice of making space in solitude prepared the way for my next spiritual practice: silence.

PRACTICING THE PRACTICE

The next time you have a moment to yourself, set a timer for five minutes and try sitting in a simple, upright chair in a quiet room. Or take a brief walk. If the night is clear, I personally enjoy stepping outside for a few moments in the evening to enjoy the stars.

Focus on breathing in and out, taking slow, deep breaths. We'll cover contemplative prayer practices soon enough, but for now, experiment with short moments of solitude.

Add to the time if you can. Consider when you can embrace solitude at other moments throughout your day, such as while sitting in the school pickup line, driving to work, making a meal, or folding laundry.

Afterward, consider how you felt about being in solitude and how your body reacted. If your mind is full of afflicting or distracting thoughts, consider adding some Examen questions to your day.

Don't worry about making progress or having a spiritual epiphany. Simply focus on quieting yourself before God in solitude and leaving the rest in God's hands. In the coming chapters, I'll add some prayer practices that can be used in times of silence.

SEVEN

Be Quiet

Lord, We Just . . . Need to Be Silent

Silence is the home of the word. Silence gives strength and fruitfulness to the word. We can even say that words are meant to disclose the mystery of the silence from which they come.

—HENRI NOUWEN

I SPENT MY CHILDHOOD wandering a little patch of woods behind my grandparents' home. In college I frequented a field near campus as a refuge from the noise of my dorm. When I entered the "real world" of adulthood, however—with graduate school, a job, children, and plenty of bills—I relegated the regular practices of solitude and silence to my past. Sure, kids and college students have time to wander in the woods, but it's another matter for an adult to drop everything for a period of solitary silence.

The complex truth, though, is that while I prioritized taking time for myself during college, I was far from silent or contemplative during my wanderings in that field. If anything, I was desperate for God to show up and offer proof for his existence. I wanted a spiritual poke from time to time, to just reassure me that yes, God is real. Years after those anxious walks, I finally began to face my anxiety and spiritual emptiness. I didn't exactly crave the silence of solitude; rather, I crash-landed into these practices. It was pure desperation to tame my mind, which could so easily spin out of control with worries, anger, or fears about the future, that led me to silence. Only when I became aware of my anxiety did I turn to silence as a refuge. I needed the practice of the Examen—not to mention the timely prayers of others—to help snap me out of the downward spiral of inward anxiety that raged unchecked.

Without the guidance of contemplative writers and the ancient prayer practices they taught me, I may have turned to other sources of comfort and medication. Entertainment and alcohol are two of the most common medications offered in our noisy, anxious culture. The ongoing noise of our entertainment- and news-saturated culture can produce either a numbing or frantic effect in us.

Many churches fail to see how much we are suffering from the inundation of noise and information. If anything, many churches are fighting fire with fire, adding more noise and information by cranking up the music, creating more courses, and stepping up the production of sermons with bigger sound systems and video clips. Rather than helping us value the silence, in which we may hear God's still, small voice, churches can add to the noise.

As we are consumed with the problems of our world and our personal lives, Christians are often given only more information, activity, and words to say. We are encouraged to keep our minds operating at full capacity instead of giving ourselves a moment to hear God say, "Be still, and know that I am God!" (Psalm 46:10). Henri Nouwen goes as far as to suggest that relying on our words or the words of others reveals a struggle to trust God. "Sometimes it seems that our many words are more an expression of our doubt than of our faith," he writes. "It is as if we are not sure that God's Spirit can touch the hearts of people: we have to help him out and, with many words, convince others of his power."[1] We surround ourselves with words because we fear the doubts and uncertainties that could arise in silence. We may even doubt that God will lead us to where we need to go.

But God may just surprise you when you create the space for silence. Thomas Merton writes:

The ears with which one hears the message of the Gospel are hidden in man's heart, and these ears do not hear anything unless they are favored with a certain interior solitude and silence. In other words, since faith is a matter of freedom and self-determination—the free receiving of a freely given gift of grace—man cannot assent to a spiritual message as long as his mind and heart are enslaved by automatism. He will always remain so enslaved as long as he is submerged in a mass of other automatons, without individuality and without their rightful integrity as persons.[2]

Silence doesn't have to be a major pilgrimage into the wilderness. Everyday tasks such as driving around town, folding laundry, preparing food, washing dishes, or taking walks can all provide a measure of silence each day. To be contemplative in nature, these tasks have to be approached with the right mindset and a commitment to shut off televisions, computers, tablets, phones, radios, and anything else that could interrupt silence.

While prayer depends on removing distractions so that God can move in us, there are more than enough things to keep us distracted today. We live in a time of unprecedented distraction that can prevent us from truly entering into the rest of prayer. If roughly 90 percent of six hundred Christians say that their greatest struggle in prayer is distracting thoughts, as my readers mentioned to me, then perhaps you can relate to this struggle.

When I've been more intentional about my spiritual practices and reading, my mind slips much more readily into prayer. Everything is connected. A quiet, solitary spirit is cultivated rather than discovered. By the same token, when I'm immersed in current events, sports, or the latest social media spat, I'm far more likely to spend my solitary time lamenting certain decisions, dreading something in the future, or rigorously justifying myself. Once I am aware of what has been on my mind and have established ways to respond in faith with a particular prayer, sacred word, or silence before God, my anxious thoughts lose a great deal of their power.

Silence is often most beneficial when linked with sustained spiritual practices of mindfulness, prayerful intention, and restful meditation or centering prayer. Over time, silence becomes all the more desirable because we see the benefits of silence and the spiritual practices that go with it. While it's obvious that intentional time away for a retreat, whether for a few hours or days, can bring great benefit, that is no substitute for seeking out pockets of silence each day.

TYRANNY OF THE DEVICE

When are we completely unplugged from information and technology these days? When are we sheltered from the noise? We can convince ourselves that everything is urgent, from a household chore to our email—which we just checked a few minutes ago but refresh one more time just in case. There's always something else to say. Henri Nouwen writes, "We have become so contaminated by our wordy world that we hold to the deceptive opinion that our words are more important than our silence."[3]

For many of us, that kind of silence happens only in the shower. If your mind isn't spinning with worries and fears and plans, you may even have a stereotypical eureka moment in the shower. Given a little unoccupied space to operate, our minds can surprise us as they process the material on hand and catch up with the events of each day. Perhaps the promise of a few untangled thoughts may be enough to help us value more silence each day.

My own pursuit of silence has largely depended on removing as many distractions as possible from my home and from the devices I use. For me, this has meant removing most social media apps from my phone. Our phones are designed to be user-friendly distraction machines that generate revenue. It shouldn't surprise us that these devices, which can sometimes make life easier, are also supposed to make themselves appear essential.

Even if I turn off every possible notification on my phone, I can still fill many spare moments in my day with swipes through my email or the news instead of seizing a few minutes or seconds for a quiet moment before God. It is significantly easier to waste fifteen minutes or more flipping through news, social media, and updates than to face the emptiness of silence and solitude. Even when I remind myself that I never regret a quiet moment with God, the lure of easy distraction or entertainment is hard to defeat.

I don't drive five minutes to the store without my phone these days. Today, a reported 68 percent of teen drivers text while the car is in motion, and half of the remaining 32 percent turn to their phones like hungry wolves when they pause at a stop sign or red light.[4] I have had several close calls with drivers who rolled up to a stop sign and started texting as I began to walk across the intersection. They had no idea that they were about to crash into me until I shouted and ran out of the way. Ironically, we bring our cell phones so that we feel safer in the car, but we end up becoming a greater menace to ourselves and to others. I can't help wondering if there's a greater lesson here about our use of technology today. Do our phones promise connection but leave us more disconnected? Do our phones promise to make us feel put together but leave us more fragmented?

Besides our mobile distractions, our homes are also filled with distractions that make it even harder to choose silence. When a television stands at the center of many living spaces and our habitual impulse is to turn it on when entering the room, there's little chance we'll have the discipline to shut it off and spend five minutes, let alone twenty, in quiet contemplation. Our public spaces are filled with flat-screen televisions and other screens that save us from our own thoughts or any measure of silence. Advertisements fill our magazines, sports arenas, websites, and every popular entertainment medium. I wrote in my book *First Draft Father* about the preposterous promotions at hockey games that involve throbbing music and throwing food into stands full of people who are already stuffed with pretzels, hot dogs, and popcorn from the concession stands. I was concerned about taking my children into the chaos of this over-the-top, consumer-driven atmosphere. Two years later, I took my son to a hockey game. Sure enough, during one of these promotions, a pizza box landed right on his head.

No one can make a dollar from a consumer who is content in silence. Before the spread of computers, smartphones, and tablets, Thomas Merton wrote, "What we must do is begin by unlearning our wrong ways of seeing, tasting, feeling, and so forth, and acquire a few of the right ones. For asceticism is not merely a matter of renouncing television, cigarettes, and gin. Before we can begin to be ascetics, we first have to learn to see life as if it were something more than a hypnotizing telecast."[5] Silence helps us unplug from the telecast—not to mention the constant stream of information and advertisements that characterizes modern life.

When I realized just how many forces try to grab my attention each day for the sake of making a sale, I became more guarded in how I viewed media and what kinds of things I allowed myself to see each day. In 2005 we gave away our television, which was never hooked up to cable in the first place, and we have made bookshelves the focal points of our rooms ever since. These subtle signals in our daily lives can determine how we spend our time each day. Yet it's still a challenge to choose moments of quiet or to find time to be alone before God.

Checking my phone for the forty-ninth time today isn't going to help my soul become more aware of God's presence. In fact, I've removed most of the apps on my phone, with the exception of the apps and websites that help with prayer. There's nothing like pulling out your phone while waiting in line for a bit of a distraction and realizing, "Oh, right . . . prayer. I should get on that." Unfortunately, there are still times when I'll have no option available other than prayer . . . and I still have to make myself choose prayer.

While silence is something we can learn to value and even crave, it doesn't happen by accident. It calls for intention and discipline, which are supported by simple spiritual practices.

SILENCE FREES US TO SERVE OTHERS

I'm an introvert who grew up in a family with quite a few extroverts. I spent years wondering what was wrong with me. Why did I find small talk so excruciating when meeting new people? Why did I run out of words when many around me appeared energized by conversation? Even worse, my forced attempts at conversation sometimes resulted in making odd, awkward, or off-topic remarks. As a conversation would begin to nosedive, I had an incredible knack for following up with something that somehow made things worse. Rather than being comfortable in my own skin and keeping my mouth shut when others argued, I sometimes ventured into arguments that I had no business joining. Other times I tried to lighten the mood and made jokes that offended people who were very important to me. I have seen firsthand how careless words can cause plenty of trouble.

As I have learned to accept my limitations around conversations and small talk, I have stopped worrying about being quiet. I have stopped worrying that people will consider me rude if I don't have much of anything to say. When I'm in a large group, I'm content to have a few deep conversations without feeling the burden to engage everyone. Most importantly, I've cut down on the number of awkward or damaging conversations I've had.

At the same time that I learned to value silence in social settings, I became more comfortable with silent prayer. As my social anxiety decreased, my embrace of silence in prayer also led to unexpected changes in the way I pray. The movement toward silence involves two essential steps: removing ourselves from noise and keeping ourselves from contributing to the noise.

While we can't always control the amount of noise in our surroundings, we can certainly control what comes out of our mouths. Silence can serve several purposes: pulling us away from the controversies of our times, keeping us from offending others, and making us more available for God. Thomas Merton wrote of the desert fathers: "If these men say little about God, it is because they know that when one has been somewhere close to His dwelling, silence makes more sense than a lot of words.

The fact that Egypt, in their time, was seething with religious and intellectual controversies was all the more reason for them to keep their mouths shut."[6]

How many stories in the Bible introduce us to people who were close to God . . . and then blundered badly when they spoke up? Many come to mind: Moses doubting God at the burning bush (Exodus 3), Elijah arguing with God at Mount Horeb (1 Kings 19), Peter's off-topic offer to build booths on Mount Tabor (Matthew 17). The prophet Habakkuk contrasted idols to the God of Israel with this final conclusion: "But the Lord is in his holy temple; let all the earth keep silence before him!" (2:20).

In addition, our words can often get us into trouble because they create vicious cycles of entanglement with controversy or offense. These controversies and offenses occupy time in our minds and hearts, and our dwelling on these entanglements only further disrupts us and leads to additional arguments and offenses. Silence is one of the ways that we guard our hearts as we go about our day. Silence helps place our trust entirely in God to renew our hearts and minds in prayer.

The problem isn't that we desire to speak. Rather, it's that we speak before we have become grounded in God's loving presence or, in some cases, received direction from God. Moses and Elijah were eager to speak, and God intended for them to use their voices for the benefit of others. The trouble was that they were talking first, preventing themselves from hearing God. Once they were silent long enough to hear from God, they knew what to say—and what not to say. Those who move forward solely on their wisdom are in danger of misusing their words.

Jesus didn't hold back in his evaluation of the words coming from the hearts of the Pharisees and scribes:

Either make the tree good, and its fruit good; or make the
tree bad, and its fruit bad; for the tree is known by its fruit.
You brood of vipers! How can you speak good things, when
you are evil? For out of the abundance of the heart the
mouth speaks. The good person brings good things out of a
good treasure, and the evil person brings evil things out of an
evil treasure. I tell you, on the day of judgment you will have
to give an account for every careless word you utter; for by
your words you will be justified, and by your words you will
be condemned. (Matthew 12:33-37)

Seen in conjunction with the words received by Abba
Arsenius—flee, be silent, pray—silence becomes a tool of transformation. Rather than seeing silence as merely a barricade that
prevents us from sinning (James 3:1-12), we can see silence
as freeing us from the entanglements of slander, offense, arguments, deception, and angry words. The less entangled we are,
the better prepared we are to be present for God and to speak
life-giving words when appropriate. Father Poemen shared, "If
you are silent, you will have peace wherever you live."[7]

In silence, I must face what kind of person I truly am. Rather
than using my words to project a kind of ideal self, I must tell
the truth of who I am. Since learning to be comfortable with
silence, I have become more aware of the people around me and
can respond more productively to what they are saying. Silence
also helps me stop defending my false self. It enables me to face
the stark reality that my soul has so far to go to fully rest in God.
When I am at peace in God, my words will come from a place
of security and I will be freed up to be more aware of others.

In silence before God, I have found that I can't rely on
my own words to make my own spiritual formation happen.

Whatever happens during a period of silence is a gracious gift from God. Whatever I receive from God becomes a gift that I can freely share with others. That is not a small matter. The more that spiritual formation depends on my own words, effort, and wisdom, the less grace I'll have for others. If other people aren't "advancing spiritually," I may be tempted to think they aren't as good at spiritual formation as I am. But silence teaches me that we all have access to the same grace, mercy, and transformation from God. The difference from one person to another is time and space. We all have the capacity to keep silent. We all have the capacity to find time each day for God. Spiritual formation often becomes a matter of how much space we leave for God to work in our lives.

As I've learned to stop obsessing about the way I present myself with my words or how I can use my words to grow spiritually, my defensiveness of my false self has started to dissolve. Mind you, old habits are hard to break. I can only hope and pray that ten or twenty years from now, I'll have an even greater awareness of God's mercy and the needs of those around me. But I can only move closer to God and to others if I intentionally create space for silence each day. Each day the choice of silence is a greater struggle than I think it should be. The pull of distractions and the seeming wisdom of my own words and thoughts remain alluring.

SILENCE ISN'T AN ACCIDENT

In my own movement from anxious evangelical spirituality to secure practices of silence and contemplation before God, I've had to build new habits. I've had to create certain points each day that are reserved for prayer, silence, or a measure of solitude. These changes didn't happen overnight. I spent far too long struggling to remain silent for five minutes. I had to re-move many distractions from my life so that silent prayer be-fore God became more automatic rather than a last resort when anxiety got the best of me.

My defaults over the years have been distractions for my leisure time, from watching sports to turning current events into a kind of sport, and spirituality had more to do with what I said or studied. The disciplines of solitude and silence are not natural, especially with so many inviting distractions and so many urgent topics that demand a response from us.

While silence always requires a measure of planning and in-tention, it gets easier. After a season of practicing silence regu-larly, it becomes more natural. I have started to recognize the times I need to step back for a moment of quiet contemplation, resting in silence before God and trusting God to be present.

Taking a deep breath in and out can signal my intention to be still for a moment. I can take this deep breath while sitting at a red light or while scrubbing a pile of dishes. Some days I continue breathing deeply—in and out, over and over again— as part of my intention to pray in silence. Other days I'll turn to a simple prayer, phrase, or sacred word to guide my prayer practice (we'll discuss that in the next chapter). I may simply call on the name of Jesus. I might say the Jesus Prayer ("Lord Jesus Christ, Son of God, have mercy on me, a sinner"). Or I might recite a brief Scripture, such as "Speak, Lord, for your servant is listening" (1 Samuel 3:9).

It can feel a little odd to "learn" how to be silent. Shouldn't being quiet, by ourselves, come naturally? In theory, yes. But silence is the kind of thing you can lose if you stop practicing it. I'm far more likely to pursue distractions or to put myself at the mercy of my environment in order to avoid being silent by myself. It's still so easy to succumb to the search for something to stream on my computer or to the vapid infinite scrolling of social media sites. In fact, the more I faced myself without the smokescreen of these distractions, the less I liked myself. This is the encounter with the fragile false self, or imposter, that so many contemplatives write about. For many, that encounter alone may be the greatest barrier to solitude and silence. To get to the other side of silence, you have to confront what the noise of life is hiding.

This is why silence is ideally situated within Christian spiritual practices such as contemplative prayer, in which God's love and mercy call us away from our distractions and explanations. My perspective on silence changed when I realized that I'm not putting myself at the mercy of my worst fears about myself when I'm alone. In silence, I'm putting myself at the mercy of God. God alone can repair my worst thoughts about myself. God alone can heal my fragile ego, which I am tempted to defend at all costs.

WHATEVER THOUGHTS FLOAT YOUR BOATS

Distractions and wandering thoughts are inevitable during silence and prayer. There may well be a time when a particularly compelling thought is the Spirit nudging you to resolve something before pursuing prayer. The principle is similar to this teaching of Jesus: "So when you are offering your gift at the altar, if you remember that your brother or sister has something against you, leave your gift there before the altar and go; first be reconciled to your brother or sister, and then come and offer your gift" (Matthew 5:23-24).

When our mouths stop moving and we enter into silence, our minds can really kick into high gear. We have trained our bodies to crave motion to the point that stopping physically is only a signal to put our minds into motion. The challenge of silence, especially silent prayer that intends to be present for God, is to pair audible silence with mental silence as well.

Thomas Keating compares distracting thoughts to boats floating through one's consciousness. While practicing any kind of contemplative prayer, let each thought pass by instead of jumping on the "boat" and riding it downstream. The distractions (or "boats") will come, no matter how isolated and silent we become. The learned discipline of silent prayer is to develop the strength to let distracting thoughts go. This strength resists the urge to hold on to these thoughts.

We can't fight distracted thinking with another kind of distracted thinking. Richard Rohr writes that in contemplative prayer, we surrender rather than fight. He adds that this surrender doesn't come naturally: "The 'how' of letting go is so counter to ego consciousness that it has to be directly taught, and it can only be taught by people who know the obstacles and have experienced surrender as the path to overcoming them. The contemplative mind, which is really prayer itself, is not subject to a mere passing on of objective information. *It must be practiced and learned*, just like playing the piano or basketball."[8]

I have had to take ownership of my anxious thoughts and fears, recognizing their presence, breathing deeply, and then gently returning to silence or prayer. Thomas Merton describes the Christian contemplative prayer tradition as passed down from the desert fathers as a restful act: "What we would call contemplative prayer today is referred to as *quies* or 'rest.' This illuminating term has persisted in Greek monastic tradition as *hesychia*, 'sweet repose.'"[9] Engaging in a battle against my thoughts, or chastising myself for praying badly, undermines the intention of resting in God's presence. It is humbling to re-alize that I need to practice how to rest in a life-giving, focused manner. The difference between those who are experienced in this kind of prayer and those who are not is the degree of their awareness of God's loving presence. God remains fully present for all and is equally delighted at the desire of all to pray.

Interrupting thoughts will always distract us from prayer, but we can gain greater control over our thoughts, manage them better throughout the day, and let go of them more ef-fectively. I haven't arrived, but I am learning to be mindful of my thoughts, to recognize when my thinking is not in a healthy place, and to stop myself in order to pray. Again, anxious evan-gelicals can make the mistake of focusing on ways to "improve" at contemplative prayer. But God's Spirit is already in us. We can't improve on God's presence. We can only improve on being present for God, turning away from our distractions.

When I began to practice contemplative prayer, I already had everything from God I would ever need. The "results" of contemplative prayer are more or less imperceptible as I gently let my thoughts go and return to a sacred word so that God can work. There really is nothing to measure here. There is no ru-bric by which contemplative practitioners can rank themselves. The heart of contemplative prayer truly rests in what God is doing in us.

Over time, I have seen the benefits of solitude and silence. I have begun to crave a little time in my room by myself, with the door shut. I can now sense when life has worn me down or my mind has been upended by the events of the day. That doesn't mean I'm always successful at seeking or even finding silence when I need it most. But I am now aware of my mental and spiritual state each day. Silence has helped me learn to recognize when I am off-center. The pursuit of solitude and silence before God has become a refuge rather than something to dread. In solitude and silence, I have found the space to move beyond praying in my own words.

Some have called this type of silent prayer before God the "prayer of the heart." One of the most commonly used paths toward contemplation has been the practice of centering prayer, which is enfolded within silence and finds its true home there.

PRACTICING THE PRACTICE

In your conversations and interactions with others over the next few days, pay attention to what you are inclined to say. Pause before saying anything. Consider some of these questions:

- Am I really hearing the other person?
- Am I trying to project a certain image of myself?
- Could I hold on to my thoughts for a moment without verbalizing them?
- Is it possible my words don't add as much to a conversation as I had hoped? How does that make me feel?

If you are already seeking solitude, what kinds of thoughts pass through your mind? Are there things you could change about your day to create more quiet in your mind? How can you make more space for silence today?

EIGHT

Begin with Intention

Learning Centering Prayer

*A naked intent direct to God is sufficient
without anything else.*

—FROM *THE CLOUD OF UNKNOWING*

CENTERING PRAYER is an ancient Christian practice that can be traced back to the desert fathers and mothers. Passed down through monasteries, centering prayer has been reintroduced to wider audiences through many Catholic and a few Protestant writers in recent times. At the heart of centering prayer is a sacred word, such as *beloved* or *mercy* or *Jesus*, or a centering action, such as deep breathing, that offers a resting place when thoughts come to mind. When we begin centering prayer, we are creating a space for communion with God in contemplative prayer. Thomas Merton warns us that the search for God can be easily subverted: "Another law of the contemplative life is that if you enter it with the set purpose of seeking contemplation, or worse still, happiness, you will find neither."[1]

Centering prayer leads us toward a greater awareness of God. As opposed to a mantra, which may leave us empty or in a kind of trance, centering prayer removes distractions so that we can be available for God. For a time I was suspicious of centering prayer because of its alleged ties to New Age movements or Eastern religions, but I soon learned that it is a historically rooted Christian practice. Understanding the unique character of centering prayer and its centrality in the Christian tradition has proven helpful when I explain it to my fellow anxious evangelicals. Thomas Keating, in the foreword to Cynthia Bourgeault's *Centering Prayer and Inner Awakening*, distinguishes between "the basic receptivity of Centering Prayer and the concentrative character of mindfulness practices in other spiritual traditions, both Eastern and Western." He adds that centering prayer, "inspired by the tradition of the Desert Fathers and Mothers, emphasizes purity of heart, which is a disposition of humility and pure love leading to total self-surrender. Indeed, to distinguish Centering Prayer from practices of concentrative attention, we might call it 'heartfulness' practice."[2]

So what does this "heartfulness" practice look like? How can we practice it in the middle of our distracted, busy lives? As a kind of spoiler alert, keep in mind that the ultimate destination for centering prayer is the love of God, not a mountaintop epiphany.

INTENTION AT CENTER

Surrendering to the love of God stands at the heart of centering prayer, according to Cynthia Bourgeault, who has studied prayer from many religious traditions. She writes that "contemplative prayer is simply a wordless, trusting opening of self to the divine presence. Far from being advanced, it is about the simplest form of prayer there is."[3] Bourgeault notes that this intention sets it apart from other traditions: "Being clear about your intention is really the touchstone of Centering Prayer, for the method of the prayer will consist primarily of a repeated returning to and refocusing of your intention, just as one repeatedly refocuses a camera lens that has drifted slightly off."[4]

The simplicity of this prayer method is easy for anxious Christians to overthink. If you're like me, you may enter into centering prayer with an anxious desire to have every little detail spelled out. I have found that contemplative teachers often have a valid concern that their students could become too mechanical in their approach to prayer if they spell things out too explicitly. When I first learned about centering prayer, I looked for a process that delivered results. I asked, What's the method? How do I get the right results? Why didn't it work right? I ran right past the importance of setting up a "naked intent" toward God as my foundation. Intention is our starting point, and the only focal point in centering prayer. With this simple intention in place, my anxious measurements for success were preemptively shut down. While the mind can wander aimlessly all day or shift from one distraction to another, centering prayer offers us a simple way to be lovingly present for God.

A simple prayer word may be all that we need to be fully present. Many of the desert fathers and mothers spent their days reciting the prayer of the repentant tax collector: "Have mercy on me, a sinner." That prayer has since been expanded into the Jesus Prayer, which many Catholic monks and people in other Christian traditions use to this day: "Lord Jesus Christ, Son of God, have mercy on me, a sinner."

Whether those practicing contemplation use the Jesus Prayer, a simple phrase, a single word, or even just regular breathing, centering prayer has continued more or less without interruption since the days of the desert fathers and mothers. Amid the Western church's upheavals, power plays, corruption, the Reformation, and the Counter-Reformation, contemplative prayer in the Western church was largely confined to monasteries until recent centuries. Most of the latest teachings on contemplative prayer today can be traced to a prayer book called *The Cloud of Unknowing*, which was written by a Carthusian monk in England during the 1300s to guide novices in prayer.

The Carthusians are among the most quiet and withdrawn orders, devoting themselves to solitude and prayer. It shouldn't surprise us that one of their own took the time to preserve the Christian contemplative tradition that is so central to their daily prayer practices. Today's contemplative prayer teachers—including William Meninger, Thomas Keating, Basil Pennington, and Cynthia Bourgeault—trace their teachings back to this prayer manual.

Consider what the author of the *Cloud of Unknowing* says: "[Lift] up your heart toward God with a meek stirring of love. . . . For a naked intent direct to God is sufficient without anything else. . . . And if you desire to have this aim concentrated and expressed in one word in order that you might be better able to grasp it, take but one short word of a single syllable . . . and clasp this word tightly in your heart so that it never leaves no matter what may happen."[5]

The sacred word or phrase isn't something you have to invent. I can imagine anxious Christians trying to think of the most biblical and all-encompassing sacred words: Righteousness! Holiness! Sovereignty! Majesty! But Keating directs us to ask the Spirit to guide us to a sacred word. Bourgeault goes so far as to encourage sticking with a particular sacred word for years rather than jumping around from one to another.

God's love and mercy, as well as our own belovedness as God's children, will most likely show up in the words we center on. When I began to pray centering prayers, I tentatively started centering on the word *beloved*, because it struck me as the hardest thing to believe about myself in connection to God. I struggled to move beyond a fear that I had never done—and will never do—enough for God. While leading one retreat, I led a time of *lectio divina* with Psalm 23 and then felt prompted to suggest centering on the word *shepherd*. In the years since then, I have sensed the Spirit leading me to the word *mercy*. Some teachers use the Jesus Prayer or a variation of it as a prayer word, such as *Lord, have mercy*.

You can be reasonably certain that your own voice is drowning out the Spirit if you keep thinking of sacred words that lead you to greater striving or fear of inadequacy. *Shape up* won't lead you into God's loving and gracious presence, which is the one place where we can find the hope of change and sanctification. Romans 7 has assured anxious Christians all along that our own willpower and planning are doomed to fail. Paul spells out the inner conflict that can only be resolved by surrendering to God's intervention: "For I delight in the law of God in my inmost self, but I see in my members another law at war with the law of my mind, making me captive to the law of sin that dwells in my members. Wretched man that I am! Who will rescue me from this body of death?" (Romans 7:22-24).

The teachers of centering prayer assure us that God's path to transformation runs through our hearts or souls rather than as an appeal to our minds. Believe me, I've tried both. I can't learn or will myself into God's holiness, but my own willpower and planning can make all the difference in whether I am present for God and his transformation. I have long worried that I wasn't able to make a spiritual transformation happen in my life, but the actual work of transformation is God's alone. My own role in centering prayer is to make myself still and to direct my intentions toward God's love so that God can work in my soul. Bourgeault assures us, "Your own subjective experience of the prayer may be that nothing happened—except for the more-or-less continuous motion of letting go of thoughts. But in the depths of your being, in fact, plenty has been going on, and things are quietly but firmly being rearranged."[6]

Of course we are still responsible for our moral choices, but Jesus' message focused on fulfilling the law out of love, not willpower. I have wondered if my struggle for spiritual transformation can be traced to lacking both the language and the practices that could lead toward a loving, transformative union with God.

THE JOURNEY TOWARD CENTERING PRAYER

Centering prayer has traditionally been taught through a spiritual director who helps others through their spiritual journeys by listening and asking questions over a series of regular meetings. The books by Thomas Keating and Cynthia Bourgeault have proven revolutionary in part because they have succeeded in directing readers through spiritual practices with simple, accessible language. While I often tell those interested in contemplative practices, such as centering prayer, to seek out a spiritual director, a friend familiar with the practices, or a retreat dedicated to contemplative practices, reading about the experiences and steps that others have taken can be helpful when starting out with centering prayer. When these practices were first taking root in my life, I was especially blessed to attend a church filled with spiritual directors and people practicing contemplative prayer. It was immensely helpful to ask questions as I integrated the ancient prayer practices of the church into my life. As a way of recapping the journey of this book up to this point and tying it all together, here is a brief overview of my journey into contemplative practices like daily silence and centering prayer. Perhaps this will help you sort out the steps in your own path.

Before I sought out the simplicity of centering prayer, I first learned to pray with Scripture by meditating on smaller passages, often a single verse from the Psalms. This daily meditation on Scripture grew as I learned to pray with Scripture more regularly through the set times, or morning, noon, and vespers in the divine hours. These were crucial steps toward centering prayer because my own voice no longer dominated my prayer time. I was resting with the words of Scripture, often waiting for a passage from the day's Scripture readings to stand out to me.

Mind you, my thoughts were still quite active while praying with Scripture. I hadn't yet embraced a prayer practice like centering prayer, which is defined by silence and communing with God internally. My prayer was still mostly meditative and active. Yet I needed that small win of making myself "less active" while praying. I took small steps toward centering prayer as I clumsily prayed the Jesus Prayer from time to time or recited the Our Father. Reciting the prayers of others from the daily office also helped me move away from my wordy, anxious prayers.

As I learned more about resting in God's presence in prayer, I found the Examen and began using it as a way to clear my mind before sitting in silence for five minutes. Those five minutes were agonizing, but they were more bearable if I processed my thoughts through the Examen first. Taking regular walks or running also served as a kind of Examen and experience of solitude over the years so that I could become more aware of my thoughts. When I finally began to practice silence and centering prayer, I had a stronger foundation of restful prayer that didn't hinge on my own words. I had a better grasp of how to embrace silence and then let go of my thoughts.

PRACTICING CENTERING PRAYER

The ideal practice for centering prayer is a time of at least twenty minutes of solitude, sitting upright in a comfortable position. I certainly aim for that whenever possible. Spiritual directors typically advise praying first thing in the morning. As a parent with kids who wake up early and then need a nap, I have found afternoons to be the most viable time. I'm sure that will change soon enough. I still incorporate the fixed-hour prayers of the divine hours into my day whenever possible, using a reminder on my phone, because they help reorient my thoughts so that centering prayer isn't such a shock to the system.

Centering prayer is not an out-of-body experience or spiritual epiphany. It often feels like a bit of work—and a bit of rest—as I try to let go of my body's tension and thoughts before settling into my sacred word. I let go of one thought after another. Sometimes that gets easier as I rest in God's mercy. Entering into this prayer time, I remind myself that my intention is one of love for and surrender to a loving God. It's even better if I can carry that intention and surrender throughout my day as I work and spend time with my family. Martin Laird is insistent that deep, cleansing breaths can prove especially important for a restful time of centering prayer. In fact, the Jesus Prayer was typically tied with deep breathing—breathing in "Jesus Christ," and breathing out "Son of God," and so forth. Laird warns us, "Shallow, short breathing is often resistance to deep, ungrasping stillness and can mask personal issues in the unconscious that have not been met."[7]

I can't emphasize enough that I rarely see spectacular results in the moment. I was addicted to results for so long that I still feel that I'm a failure at prayer some days. The "results" of centering prayer have been far more gradual and, not surprisingly, far more lasting and significant. For starters, I'm slowly developing an awareness of how to rest before God throughout my day. When I have a spare moment to rest in the Jesus Prayer or my sacred word, I am learning to take it. Bourgeault describes the "results" of centering prayer like this:

> Centering Prayer is not about accessing sublime states of consciousness or having mystical experiences. The fruits of this prayer are first seen in daily life. They express themselves in your ability to be a bit more present in your life, more flexible and forgiving with those you live and work with, more honest and comfortable in your own being. These are the real signs that the inner depths have been touched and have begun to set in motion their transformative work.[8]

The most striking "result" of regularly practicing centering prayer has come in the moments when I experience conflict or suffer a wound to my ego. Spiritual writers such as Richard Rohr and Brennan Manning address the false self or imposter that we all construct and then defend. This false self loses its power through centering prayer because it is overshadowed by the powerful presence of God's love, even if we can't (or perhaps even shouldn't) put it into words. Henri Nouwen writes, "When we cling to the results of our actions as our only way of self-identification, then we become possessive and defensive and tend to look at our fellow human beings more as enemies to be kept at a distance than as friends with whom we share the gifts of life."[9]

Centering prayer is not a battle against the false self. Evangelicals in particular would be the first ones to volunteer to battle the false self, just as we battle everything from lust to body image. My false self has a great deal to teach me about my own insecurities and the places where God wants to bring healing. The teachers of contemplative prayer assure us that the path to healing and holiness is what we pursue rather than what we fight against. I have found this to be true. Centering prayer has brought healing in ways that I couldn't have chosen for myself. Resting in my place as God's beloved child can do that.

Remember Thomas Keating's image of distracting thoughts as boats floating through your consciousness? For those who have jumped onto the "boat" of a particular thought, the best way to abandon ship is to return to the sacred word. Anxious Christians who want to get contemplative prayer "right" may take this a little far. We are supposed to return to the sacred word gently, but some may really beat themselves up over a failure to focus. For a season, I more or less walked the plank of each thought, lamenting how badly I was "failing" at contemplative prayer. Once I started thinking a thought, I began to think about how bad I was at not thinking thoughts—which of course was just another way of thinking about a thought. And so the downward spiral into negative thinking continued. With my intention to pray in place, I made the mistake of putting too much on myself while praying. Michael Molinos shares: "Your imagination may ramble over an infinite number of thoughts, yet, I assure you, the Lord has not left. Continue your perseverance in prayer. Remember that He prays within you, and He prays in spirit and in truth. The distraction of the mind—which is not intended—does not rob the prayer of its fruit."[10]

Keating is insistent with his use of gentleness here: *gently* return to your sacred word when distracting thoughts come. I don't even think I grasped what gentleness meant for prayer. I spent so many years trying to be a prayer warrior who battled through prayer. I had a hard time applying rest and gentleness to my prayer practices. Most times, my negative thoughts were a byproduct of my performance-driven spirituality, in which I had to prove myself or earn God's approval or presence in some way. When God's love and acceptance became the starting point for my spirituality, rest and gentleness became possible. The author of the *Cloud of Unknowing* compares these invasive, distracting thoughts to a pair of chatty sisters who repeatedly barge into your home for a visit.[11] If a reclusive Carthusian monk from the 1300s had to manage intrusive thoughts when he sought to pray, then we can only imagine the work we have in front of us today.

For all the small steps I've taken into centering prayer, I've certainly had my share of struggles along the way. If this practice appears daunting or continues to elude you, you are most certainly not alone, and there are plenty of reasons to continue pressing on.

TRANSFORMED BY LOVE AND GENTLENESS

Perhaps the most promising element of centering prayer for anxious Christians is the possibility of union with God and the resulting transformation. I grew up among conservative Christians who loved to talk about becoming holy or, to put a finer point on it, "not sinning." Anything that could help us not sin was appealing. However, many of the spiritual tools or discipleship methods we've been offered rely a great deal on willpower. Centering prayer completely disarms our best plans for spiritual change. Centering prayer helps us walk a fine line between finding the personal discipline to pray and trusting God with all the responsibility for transformation.

I am powerless to alter my spiritual condition, but I am responsible for how I use my time. God's indwelling Spirit cries out "Abba, Father" whether I am aware of it or not. However, I can miss out on the life-changing impact of that powerful presence if I never stop to acknowledge it or fail to become present for it.

When Paul wrote that the kingdom of God is a matter of power, he didn't have our own willpower in mind. As the Corinthian church continued to argue and divide, Paul gave them a choice: Would they rather he minister to them out of God's love or come after them with a rod? "For the kingdom of God depends not on talk but on power. What would you prefer? Am I to come to you with a stick, or with love in a spirit of gentleness?" (1 Corinthians 4:20-21). I have been slow to notice the power of God's transforming love in a passage like this.

Let's face it: as an anxious evangelical, I primarily preferred the discipline of the rod. I was so fearful of falling into sin or compromise that I didn't want to be perceived as being less committed or disciplined. Among some of my evangelical peers who put a premium on defending the truth or aggressively sharing the gospel, being too loving or gentle can be perceived as a risk greater than resting in God's love and letting the power of the Spirit work in our lives for transformation.

For years I lived the "Holy Spirit Lite" version of Christianity. I lacked an understanding of spiritual formation, the transforming power of God's love, and a daily spirituality that made room for the Holy Spirit. Over the years, evangelical leaders like Dallas Willard and Richard Foster have been the exception to the rule of rod-wielding, try-harder exhortations of anxious Christians.

I don't harbor animosity or hard feelings toward the "try harder" Christian leaders from my past who relied more on the rod than on God's gentle spirit of love. I inherited an expression of the Christian faith that never received the practices that could have led us to rest in God. Most evangelicals and other anxious Christians have been trained to read the Bible and to pray by voicing requests or praising God because that is what previous generations passed on to them. The majority of Christians today have inherited a severely depleted prayer tradition thanks to the mistakes made by some in the medieval church, the Reformation, and the Counter-Reformation when most Western Christians moved away from contemplative practices. We can only control whether we'll choose to benefit today from the historical prayer practices of the church.

Even if I can convince you that centering prayer is part of your heritage as a Christian, I'll be the first to admit that it is a very counterintuitive practice. During my years steeped in evangelicalism, spirituality for me was studying, thinking, and speaking. Sitting in silence, with a clear mind, and allowing God's Spirit to imperceptibly minister to me? I'd never considered it. The pursuit of silent contemplation before God can feel like either a step backward or spiritual stagnation. After focusing on my words and my thoughts and my doctrine for so long, I struggled to see any benefit from contemplative practices. This was especially true as I started to pursue silence before God. Practices like centering prayer sent all my fear, anger, and regret rushing to the front of my mind.

Such a rush of negative thinking is normal and to be expected for beginners at centering prayer. Richard Rohr shared in an interview that our most afflicting thoughts come out during the first year of practicing contemplation.[12] There's no avoiding this. The problem all along, in fact, had been my avoidance and denial of my pain. Instead of directly addressing the pain of life, many will turn to ways to dull the pain or to at least fill the perceived emptiness of life with some measure of enjoyment or pleasure. I relied on social media, news, and sports to keep my mind occupied. Some may turn to buying new things, immersing themselves in entertainment, or indulgence with food. Those experiencing deeper, more serious pain may turn to drugs or alcohol.

The stakes couldn't be any higher when we approach contemplative prayer. I've learned that I can't hide from or outrun my pain. My only hope is to call out "Abba, Father!" as the worst parts of myself come to the surface. Most importantly, I have found that the pain and shame of my past aren't the true "me." My true self has been hidden in Christ. I am a beloved child of God with whom God is well pleased.

As I face the pain and shame tucked away in my life over the years—there always seems to be more to find!—I have become only more eager to pray. It is freeing to face my own powerlessness and to rest in God's provision. In centering prayer, I literally do nothing else except wait on God. The Scriptures say that "we walk by faith, not by sight" (2 Corinthians 5:7), and centering prayer is an ultimate act of faith. We are taking steps to remove our distracting thoughts and negative impressions of ourselves in order to rest in God. We are trusting God to work in us. We are trusting that the Spirit will supply the words we need, and that we don't have to be in charge of prayer in order for God to work.

The more I step out of the way, the more available I become for God's loving presence. That isn't to say that every prayer experience is a life-changing revelation. The deeper I've gone into this form of prayer, the more significant changes I've had to make to my expectations for prayer, especially for centering prayer. Grounding myself in the teachings of contemplative practitioners on "what happens" during prayer has gone a long way toward alleviating my anxiety.

PRACTICING THE PRACTICE

Set aside five, ten, twenty, or thirty minutes for centering prayer. Take the following steps:

1. On the first occasion, ask the Holy Spirit to guide you to a prayer word. Or consider using the Jesus Prayer.
2. Sit in an upright chair or on the floor.
3. Trust that God is love and will provide what you need as you pray.
4. Make your intention clear to God: Out of love for God, you are making yourself present.
5. Slowly take deep breaths in and out.
6. Make your breaths your main activity.
7. As thoughts come, gently use your prayer word to let them go.
8. End with the Our Father or another prayer.

NINE

Accept Mystery

God Works in the Darkness

Trust God that you are where you are meant to be.

—TERESA OF ÁVILA

WHEN I EXPERIENCED deep doubts and uncertainty about my faith over the years, I saw it as a crisis of faith. I assumed that I had departed from the approved path toward God, which was bathed in light, truth, and knowledge. Instead, I only had the darkness of my failures and faltering faith to show for all my efforts to find God. (Please note: if your "darkness" is depression or a mental illness, I am not referring to that in any way and always advocate for seeking professional help.)

As a part of a very intellectual stream of the evangelical movement that emphasized study and knowledge as a way to avoid the darkness of doubt, I was ripe for a crisis of faith at some point. Perhaps it could more aptly be called a crisis of *knowledge*. For years I thought of this darkness of doubt, uncertainty, and sin as the very thing I should fight against and avoid. I hadn't considered that the darkness of doubt had something to teach me, or that I could go through my doubts and failures to find God on the other side.

The chief end of Christianity is our union with Christ, abiding in the vine who gives us life (see John 15:1-5). Placing my faith and hope in any other conception of the Christian life— such as airtight beliefs and easy explanations for the will of God—was bound to let me down sooner or later. While doubts and uncertainties can feel like a complete collapse of faith when standing on a foundation of theology and Bible study, the intimate pursuit of Christ through silence or centering prayer isn't going to address these doubts and uncertainties in the ways that some anxious, certainty-driven Christians would hope. Perhaps to the disappointment of some, contemplative prayer is more likely to reframe how we understand the darkness of doubt. Richard Rohr writes, "When we avoid darkness, we avoid tension, spiritual creativity, and finally transformation. We avoid God, who works in the darkness—where we are not in control! Maybe that is the secret: relinquishing control."[1] I mean, the book that helped reintroduce contemplative prayer to the Western church is titled *The Cloud of Unknowing*. You're basically just shooting a dart of love into this great big, dark mysterious cloud and then waiting . . . and waiting.

All this to say: the search for God through contemplative prayer is hardly a walk in the park. In fact, the deeper I have gone into this Christian practice, the more I've realized just how unprepared I am and how easily my expectations can lead me astray. It's hard enough to enter into the still silence of prayer. But facing the unknown darkness of the soul, trusting that God's light is shining somewhere? These are challenges that can stretch our faith beyond what we perceive to be the breaking point. Even if we clear our schedules for prayer, clear away distracting thoughts, and gently settle on a restorative prayer word, our expectations for contemplative prayer and its unknown challenges can become some of our greatest obstacles.

UNREALISTIC EXPECTATIONS

If your anxiety about prayer is anything like my own, you'll spend a lot of time overanalyzing what happened or didn't happen during prayer. At the end of a contemplative prayer time I sometimes obsess over my "results." Heck, even while praying

I have found myself critiquing and analyzing what's happening. Thomas Merton nails my tendency to analyze my prayers: "The reason why so many religious people believe they cannot meditate is that they think meditation consists in having religious emotions, thoughts, or affections of which one is, oneself, acutely aware. As soon as they start to meditate, they begin to look into the psychological conscience to find out if they are experiencing anything worthwhile. They find little or nothing. They either strain themselves to produce some interior experience, or else they give up in disgust."[2]

Contemplative prayer removes us from the driver's seat. Thomas Keating and Cynthia Bourgeault remind us of the power of our simple intentions as we enter into this prayer in order to be present for God. Bourgeault writes: "It's enough simply to reiterate Thomas Keating's reassurance that 'the only thing you can do wrong in this prayer is to get up and walk out.' To sit there and quietly continue to do the practice, even if you perceive your efforts as totally unsuccessful, is, in his words, to know what it means to 'consent to the presence and action of God within us' in whatever form it comes. The power of this prayer lies in the consent."[3]

I fought against this gentle, patient approach to prayer at first. As I began centering prayer, I wanted nothing less than a spiritual awakening, a reassurance of God's presence that I couldn't deny, and a discovery of peace and hope that revolutionized my daily life. Was that too much to ask?

Instead, I struggled to quiet my thoughts as I repeated my centering word in five-, ten-, and twenty-minute stretches. Some days I'm still challenged to clear away twenty minutes each day for this type of prayer. Author Carl McColman has written that twenty minutes is an ideal minimum, but you could try to start with a ten-minute stretch if you must. However—and this is the kicker for busy folks today—McColman adds that if you can't even manage more than ten minutes, then you really need twenty minutes!

It's true that learning contemplative prayer was far harder than I expected. I had to face a lot of pain and negativity that I had ignored or overlooked. Even now, however, it can be difficult to pray if I haven't kept up with regular soul work. So much of my mental and spiritual health can hinge on whether I've intentionally made space for a moment of solitude, entered into silence, or recentered my thoughts by practicing the Examen at some point in the day.

Even if I get all those things lined up perfectly, setting myself up for "success" when I pray, it's still quite likely that I'll sit in silence before God without perceiving a significant spiritual epiphany. That isn't to say that I never hear from God while praying, or that every time I pray I experience agonizing thoughts and darkness. God is just as likely to offer direction while I'm engaged in centering prayer as the times when I'm shopping at ALDI and hear God's voice completely out of the blue while looking for my favorite chocolate bar. Rather, each moment of silent contemplation or centering prayer is a surrender to a God who abides in a great cloud of unknowing while mysteriously working in people. Prayer is an act of consent to God and the shooting of a dart of love toward the mystery of God. How God emerges from the mystery is not for us to determine.

PRAYER WITHOUT MEASUREMENTS

Practicing centering prayer can be a lot like establishing a regular exercise routine. Progress can be slow and agonizing, often feeling more like failure than a step forward. When I started running regularly, I had to build up my strength and endurance, mainly by *not* running—settling for a brisk stroll before I could manage a sustained run. The first three to four months were pure agony. If I pushed myself too hard, I needed to either walk or cut my run short. While I was better off doing some exercise rather than none, the benefits appeared to be minimal. Only after four months of regular exercise did I notice strength, endurance, and even a desire to go out for a run. Month by month, I gradually added to my mileage and noticed that I had to work harder if I wanted to get my heart pumping. As running became less agonizing, I found mental space to let my mind rest or wander. While I can't say I crave running each day, I certainly miss it if I skip a day—or a week.

From my first attempts at centering prayer as an anxious evangelical seminary student to the present, I have felt very much like a rookie. There aren't levels or goals that we can reach in centering prayer. Teachers of centering prayer aren't big on giving numbers to validate their ministries. As far as I know, none of them tweet how many sustained hours of silence they've managed in a week with a little fist-bump emoticon after it. To some Christians, it may even appear to be setting the bar really low as they encourage practitioners to commit to the practice while trusting God with the results.

The Eastern Orthodox monks who recite the Jesus Prayer aren't eager to share the specifics of prayer. It's far too intimate and indescribable for them. Something that is indescribable and intimate doesn't lend itself to clear benchmarks and description. Most importantly, there's a palpable tension at times for contemplative authors and creators. Thomas Merton was especially aware of the potential pitfalls that writers and artists face when describing contemplation to others. He writes: "The artist may well receive the first taste of infused prayer . . . and often quite soon in their spiritual life, especially when the conditions are favorable: but, because of this tragic Promethean tendency to exploit every experience as material for 'creation,' the artist may remain there all his life on the threshold, never entering into the banquet, but always running back into the street to tell the passers-by of the wonderful music he has heard coming from inside the palace of the King!"[4]

Centering prayer may create the conditions for greater peace and clear thinking, but the actual practice of centering prayer is shrouded in mystery and aims to detach us from our illusive thoughts, especially those that create a false sense of self. Our thoughts are often the repository of our false selves where we attempt to justify and glorify ourselves. Brennan Manning writes, "The impostor has built life around achievements, success, busyness, and self-centered activities that bring gratification and praise from others."[5] We need to rely on God's loving presence rather than lean on our own understanding. Contemplation won't solve our problems or offer us happiness, but these may result because we will heal our false selves and find security in our identity in Christ. Merton writes, "For the contemplative and spiritual self, the dormant, mysterious, and hidden self that is always effaced by the activity of our exterior self does not seek fulfillment. It is content to be, and in its being it is fulfilled, because its being is rooted in God."[6]

If the ultimate aim of prayer is to unite us with God so that we desire what God desires, and our will becomes one with God's will, then the work of transformation comes from God alone. The process of breaking our attachments to this world is difficult and may look different from one person to another. One of the means by which God purifies people and teaches them to live by faith in God alone is through a dark night of the soul. While I hardly want to lay out a formula (learn prayer, go through a dark night of the soul, reach a higher spiritual state), it would be remiss of me to share about the mysterious practice of contemplative prayer and its goal of divine union without mentioning one of the means God may use to reach this end.

NAMING THE DARK NIGHT OF THE SOUL

It's not uncommon for Christians embarking on a contemplative journey to pass through a season of despair, a time in which one loses all sense of God's loving presence. Spanish mystic Saint John of the Cross, a Carmelite friar in the 1500s, described this type of spiritual experience as the "dark night of the soul." A dark night of the soul has been characterized as an emptying of conceptual meaning. The objects around us lose their significance, and God appears to be distant.[7] There is a loss of assurance of God and of heaven during a dark night. Many have reported that all spiritual comforts are removed and one's faith must be sustained by choosing to trust in God's care rather than in a sense of God's presence or direction. Some have described a dark night as a kind of spiritual depression, while others have expressed a longing for God that remains unfulfilled until the dark night ends. A dark night of the soul is different from doubts or uncertainties; it tends to be a more intense sense of alienation that can persist longer than some doubts about God or faith. Thomas Merton describes it as a "dark faith": "During the 'dark night' of faith, one must let himself be guided to reality not by visible and tangible things, not by the evidence of sense or the understanding of reason, not by concepts charged with natural hope, or joy, or fear, or desire, or grief, but by 'dark faith' that transcends all desire and seeks no human and earthly satisfaction, except what is willed by God or connected with His will."[8]

Perhaps the best-known dark night of the soul is Mother Teresa's experience of spiritual darkness, which lasted for nearly her entire ministry. Although she had several powerful visions of Christ in her youth, she soon entered into a lengthy season of God's perceived absence that lasted throughout most of her ministry. She found that her initial sweet encounters with Christ had to sustain her as she followed his direction to serve the poor. Only toward the end of her life did she make peace with the darkness and perceived separation from God. She wrote, "For the first time in this 11 years—I have come to love the darkness—for I believe now that it is a part, a very, very small part of Jesus' darkness and pain on earth. You have taught me to accept it [as] a spiritual side of 'your work.'"[9] While her letters about this dark night of the soul became a kind of scandal—especially among people like me, who had no grasp of dark nights of the soul at the time—a similar season of perceived separation from God is possible for those engaged in contemplative prayer.

Anxious Christians tend to want to fix and solve spiritual problems rather than endure them. Christian mystics such as John of the Cross, Teresa of Ávila, and Mother Teresa take a very different approach. They encourage us to ask what we can learn in the midst of the darkness, and encourage obedience and virtue regardless of how present God seems to be. Teresa of Ávila wrote, "It is presumptuous in me to wish to choose my path, because I cannot tell which path is best for me. I must leave it to the Lord, Who knows me, to lead me by the path which is best for me, so that in all things His will may be done."[10] These saints learned to trust God in the darkness, remaining faithful and committed to the Lord's commands. The perceived absence of God's presence only hardened their resolve to remain faithful and to trust that God would guide them to where they needed to go.

What do times of uncertainty have to show us? What would happen if, rather than avoiding mystery and uncertainty and spiritual despair, we anticipated and even submitted ourselves to such a season? Perhaps accepting the uncertainty of a dark night of the soul is the opportunity to submit to God's will out of obedience. François Fénelon writes to those bearing their crosses, "Do you want to experience true happiness? Submit yourself peacefully and simply to the will of God, and bear your sufferings without struggle."[11] He goes on to warn against placing too much confidence in spiritual experiences: "Hold to God alone and do not rely on anything you feel or taste or imagine. You will come to see how much safer this way is than chasing after visions and prophecies."[12] Rather than treating a dark night of the soul or a time of perceived alienation from God as a tragedy or a punishment, consider that it may be a time to perfect your dependence on God and your submission to God's will.

A FAILURE OF FAITH?

Dark nights of the soul, as well as more ordinary seasons of doubt and uncertainty, tap into the deepest fears of anxious Christians who are very afraid of losing God. Our faith defines our identity and how we interact with the world. Many of us have made many enormous life choices because of our faith—which university to attend, which classes to take, what profession to choose, which friends to make, what person to marry. Losing all of that would mean we had based our entire lives on an illusion. Even more so, we wouldn't have the comfort and direction of our faith to guide our futures. During my own season of doubt, I realized how many of my relationships are based on my evangelical faith, and that some very important relationships hinge on keeping that faith. I had already experienced severe strain in my family relationships when I left the Catholic faith. Would I now lose relationships with my evangelical friends because I could no longer talk about faith the way they did?

Sincere Christians, at least those in more conservative circles, don't expect to find God in silence, and they may be especially disturbed by a dark night of the soul. Speaking of doubts or a dark night of the soul is more than likely a sign to an anxious Christian that a profession of faith wasn't authentic or that a key doctrine didn't stick. The sense of distance from God, and the spiritual despair that can accompany it, simply isn't on our radar. As a recovering anxious evangelical, I've been among those who needed to grow a lot in this department. A spiritual depression can leave the unprepared completely unhinged.

For anxious Christians, experiencing doubts or a dark night of the soul often leads in one of two directions. For some, it is the point at which they give up on faith entirely and seek guidance and hope elsewhere, outside the church. I can understand this, as such a strong sense of spiritual alienation from God can feel like a heavy-handed or passive-aggressive act on God's part. Why wouldn't a loving God become present for those who are reaching out? It's hard to see the ways that misplaced attachments, expectations, or beliefs may be interfering with our faith, and so it can be disconcerting that God at times allows them to fail us. I can only say from my own experience that sometimes I needed to experience the failures of my spiritual plans and desires before I could find the health and life that God offered me.

It's impossible to create simple equations or explanations for such experiences, but often God is asking us to surrender something we have long held on to. Sometimes we need to see ourselves as seeds that are dying. At times we must enter into darkness in order for God's Spirit to renew us with a resurrection that looks quite unlike anything we can imagine. Rather than die this kind of spiritual death, some would rather walk away from the faith in order to maintain a sense of control and familiarity. Those who have been mistreated in religious contexts certainly have valid reasons for such skepticism. Many survivors of spiritual abuse testify to the hope that remains on the other side of doubt and mystery, but the rest of us would do well to honor the experiences of those who have gone through religious trauma.

For others, a season of doubt or a dark night of the soul actually leads to doubling down on pursuing theological certainty or seeking out adversaries who can provide an easier fight than the misplaced desires of their souls and their gnawing uncertainties. It's far easier for those heavily invested in shoring up their faith with dogmatic battles to fight the perceived threats of "social justice Christians," theological liberals, or assertive atheists than to ask whether God may be guiding them through a season of uncertainty or the darkness of spiritual doubt.

The contemplative mystics of the church, such as John of the Cross and Teresa of Ávila, offer a third way—one that affirms the central truths of the Christian creeds without denying our times of darkness and distance. The mystics believe we go through spiritual darkness as a part of our transformation, not as the end of our faith and ministry. Doubts and seasons of uncertainty are a part of one's faith. In fact, I am beginning to believe that they are essential in order for us to pursue the deeper matters of God's presence and our union with Christ.

When the bottom fell out of my faith, though, I thought that I was the only one experiencing doubts. It seemed as if every single Christian I knew was having amazing revelations from God. I, on the other hand, was just praying in an empty room, talking to the walls. Over time, however, I began to find that many of my peers had similar crises of faith or unraveling around the same time that I did—in our twenties.

I first needed to stop thinking of my spiritual life as if it were a capitalist economy that demanded incremental growth in order to be healthy. Abiding in Christ will ensure life, but it doesn't necessarily mean measurable growth. Now that I'm on the other side of my faith meltdown, I know that I am hardly in the clear of a future spiritual crisis or dark night of the soul.

Experiencing a dark night of the soul is not the same thing as having doubts about your faith, even if a dark night of the soul is filled with plenty of doubts and uncertainties. Nor is it the same thing as depression. Rather, a dark night of the soul is an emptying of our attachments to this world so that we can rely wholly on God. Catholic writer Emily Stimpson Chapman explains:

> A prerequisite for seeing God face to face is that every attachment to sin, both in our lives and in our hearts, must be broken. If we want to become saints, we have to desire only God's will. And we have to desire God's will not out of fear of hell, but rather out of love for heaven, out of love for God. Some of that breaking we do, as we learn to avoid vice and pursue virtue. But some of that breaking only God can do.

The dark night of the soul is, in part, how he does that. By seemingly withdrawing all spiritual consolations—all the little comforts and supports that typically come from pursuing a relationship with him—and allowing an almost crushing sense of abandonment to descend upon us, he purifies our desires and prepares us for heaven.[13]

A dark night of the soul may last for a short time or a long time. In fact, perhaps most jarring to some Christians is the fact that one can't set up spiritual defenses strong enough to ward off a dark night of the soul. I can't stay so close to Jesus that he won't decide to send me through a time of darkness and emptying. The only thing that I can do to help myself is to preemptively empty myself of the kinds of worldly attachments that a dark night may address. And even then, contemplative prayer places us fully before God's love and mercy. Our intention is presence and surrender. We don't get to set the spiritual agenda for God, even if we can commit to practices that help us yield to God. Several teachers of contemplative prayer suggest sitting in a room, pointing at each object, and declaring, "This has no meaning." That may appear a bit like madness at first. But considering that we live in a consumeristic society that places so much stock in our possessions, our image, and our work, there are far worse things we could do with our time! Is it any less mad to point at our social media profiles and to declare, "This is who I am!"

Losing your faith or sense of connection with God for a period of time can be extremely disorienting. It may even result in bitterness toward past spiritual leaders. So much of my anger toward the Catholic Church and, later, toward conservative evangelicalism has been rooted in a sense of being duped or betrayed. I played by their rules, and things still didn't work out as promised! When I told leaders and mentors about my struggles, they sometimes blamed me for not caring enough, not thinking enough, not praying enough, or not being committed enough.

In retrospect, I can see that our false selves—mine and the leaders' with whom I had shared my journey—were fighting each other. We were struggling to maintain some semblance of the identities we had created within a religious system. The attachments to the false self cannot endure the scrutiny of God. While it may be agonizing to let go of the false self at first, it is immensely freeing. As I've practiced contemplative prayer over the years, I've gradually let go of my false self and consequently found that I have less to fight over. After going through the darkness of doubt or the darkness of a dark night of the soul, one has no need to maintain the illusion of the false self. This may be particularly liberating for many.

FAREWELL, FALSE SELF

Contemplative prayer has brought me face-to-face, so to speak, with the attachments, anxieties, and projections of my false self. Each of us fashions an image of ourselves based on our relationships, accomplishments, and actions. My own evangelical movement fashions a kind of false self that is knowledgable about the Bible, politically conservative, confident in sharing the gospel with others at all times, and sexually pure—although that last point is negotiable if you can defend the Bible or deliver political power. The false self can tie us into certain subgroups and communities and can seem indistinguishable from our true selves. In fact, the more someone accomplishes, the harder it can be to let go of the false self. Richard Rohr describes the false self in his book *Immortal Diamond*: "Your False Self is how you define yourself outside of love, relationship, or divine union. After you have spent many years laboriously building this separate self, with all its labels and preoccupations, you are very attached to it. And why wouldn't you be? It's what you know and all you know. To move beyond it will always feel like losing or dying."[14] In other words, the more I affirm the false self through my actions, the harder it is to let go of my false self.

It's striking to think that my failures and frustrations are more likely signs of God's mercy than of God's displeasure. "Prayer is death to every identity that does not come from God," writes Brennan Manning about the false self's relationship to prayer. "The false self flees silence and solitude because they remind him of death." Manning adds:

> The impostor must be called out of hiding, accepted, and embraced. He is an integral part of my total self. Whatever is denied cannot be healed. To acknowledge humbly that I often inhabit an unreal world, that I have trivialized my relationship with God, and that I am driven by vain ambition is the first blow in dismantling my glittering image. The honesty and willingness to stare down the false self dynamites the steel trapdoor of self-deception.[15]

While contemplative prayer gradually chips away at this false self, replacing it with a more secure identity as God's beloved child, a dark night of the soul is more like the dynamite Manning describes: exploding illusions and leaving a space of emptiness where only God can reside. "During this dark night, God roots out our deepest attachments to sin and self, and the desolation that accompanies that rooting out is overwhelming and crushing," writes Emily Stimpson Chapman. "More than just a lack of consolation, this dark night plunges a soul into an abyss of darkness and nothingness, essentially revealing to us what we are without God and preparing us to not only carry our crosses, but to love our crosses and carry them joyfully in union with Christ."[16]

A dark night of the soul digs up our unhealthy attachments. The surprise for an evangelical like me is that even my religious beliefs and practices can become unhealthy attachments. This fact can be devastating for someone who has built an entire identity around a commitment to the Bible and specific theological commitments. It's one thing to read that the people surrounding Jesus who were most committed to the Hebrew Scriptures actually missed the person and message of Christ when he was with them. It's quite another thing to reckon with the reality that we could make the same mistake two thousand years later.

MERCY FOR OUR FALSE SELVES

It's at this point that I can sense some evangelicals like me may be willing to launch a full-scale attack on their false selves or imposters. What could be better than a preemptive strike on the false self? So perhaps a word of caution is in order here. Manning and Rohr are both emphatic that we must not attack the imposter or false self. Such a plea struck me as a bit soft at first. Then a look at my personal history changed my mind.

When my faith unraveled in my twenties, so much of my religious identity appeared foolish and fragile. I felt duped. I blamed my religious upbringing for failing me. The despair and fear in my own heart was coupled with the disapproval of religious leaders. On top of all that, I also felt a surge of anger that I had been given something so fragile and that I had trusted it so implicitly. My anger at myself and religious institutions wasn't even close to being contained. Rather than treating my false self with compassion and mercy, I was ready to judge. In many ways, I was trading one false self for another. As a "religion expert" who felt spiritually isolated from God, I merely changed sides on a few theology debates. But my false self remained at the fore.

Without compassion for who I had once been, I wasn't able to see where God could lead me or who I could become. Without embracing who I was, I wasn't able to show love and acceptance to others—especially those who still rigorously defended the same old boundary lines. Contemplative prayer has gradually cultivated this compassion in my own life, and it has only highlighted just how desperately I need to grow in my capacity for love and mercy.

The emptying that occurs through a dark night of the soul can help break these attachments to false sources of identity and security. The people I have met who have gone through dark nights of the soul have been among the most tender and grounded individuals I've ever met. They aren't fighting and clawing to hold on to their faith. They aren't looking for ways to prove themselves or to defend their beliefs. This kind of security isn't won through a clever argument or by repeatedly affirming a list of doctrines.

The parts of my faith that are unstable or unreliable will always give way. What is immovable and unshakable will endure, but it took a while before I could see that with clarity. I spent so much time fearing darkness and uncertainty that I didn't believe it could be the path to God. The cross shows us that the path to resurrection and new life must be preceded with death and a sense of abandonment. While God remains present, there is no denying the anguish of a cry, "My God, my God, why have you forsaken me?" (Mark 15:34).

Passing through death into life is Christian spirituality, and it makes up the bulk of what I affirm as a Christian. Yet I have spent so much time avoiding pain and darkness. Rohr writes, "We must learn to stay with the pain of life, without answers, without conclusions, and some days without meaning. That is the path, the perilous dark path of true prayer."[17] As I continue to learn how to let go of what is unstable, there is a time of emptiness and anticipation in which my trembling hands remain empty before the unknown abundance of God. What will God give in return? There is no guarantee.

This loss of control is pronounced within a dark night of the soul. There is no program or progress chart that can assure us of results or resolutions on a particular schedule. I spent years managing my spirituality through classes, study, and books. Each class or book promised results. When you are a Christian author, you promise to guide readers through a series of chapters that lead to a particular result. In the Christian publishing world, we claim that the reader should be different or changed in some way by the end of the book. Whether a book promises peace, purpose, order, or joy, we are a people who are used to results. That isn't to say that programs, studies, or concrete results are always a bad thing. But the spiritual practices of the Christian faith and deeper union with God calls us beyond these equations or expectations for predictable outcomes.

Stepping out into the mystery of God and even surrendering to a time of darkness strips away the things I rely on and trust. I have taken so many things for granted in establishing my stability and identity. However, everything that isn't from God or established with God will fall away. Naked I came into this world, and naked I will depart. Amid this loss and uncertainty, God is present.

Does every believer need to go through a dark night of the soul? I can't say for certain. But we do need intimacy with God. We need prayer. We benefit greatly from the restful practice of contemplation. We need God to reshape us into holy people. We need to be united with Christ. Many of us won't reach these places unless God sweeps away our illusions, attachments, and distractions. A dark night is one way that we can move toward intimacy and holiness.

I cannot imagine enduring a dark night of the soul that extended for years, as Mother Teresa experienced. But I have stepped into uncertainty, faced my false self, and seen my false securities stripped away. I can't say for sure whether I've gone through the same extreme spiritual experiences like other spiritual mentors I know, but I have waited in spiritual darkness and silence. All I can wait for is the loving presence of God. That is all that remains, and that is enough. If I am not satisfied with my identity as a beloved child of God, I'll forever search for substitutes that will forever let me down.

PRACTICING THE PRACTICE

As you consider that a dark night of the soul helps remove your attachments to everything that blocks your path to God, consider how a fast during the season of Lent helps you expose what you're most attached to.

What is the one thing you can't imagine doing without?

What if you deprived yourself of that one thing for a brief time, even a day or a few hours?

Pay attention to how that affects your outlook and the space you have for God.

TEN

Now What?

Alternatives to Consumer Contemplation

All desires but one can fail. The only desire that is infallibly fulfilled is the desire to be loved by God. We cannot desire this efficaciously without at the same time desiring to love Him, and the desire to love Him is a desire that cannot fail. Merely by desiring to love Him, we are beginning to do that which we desire. Freedom is perfect when no other love can impede our desire to love God.

—THOMAS MERTON

THERE IS A RISK in writing about anxious Christianity and contemplative prayer, especially in a relatively prosperous Western context that has its fair share of issues with consumer spirituality. Contemplative prayer isn't the sort of thing you sprinkle into your life to alleviate anxiety so that you can live your best life or find your purpose. The "now what?" that evangelicals like me have been trained to ask about all things spiritual is simple enough to describe, but it's challenging to apply when it comes to contemplative prayer. The goal of "flee, be silent, pray" is to become aware of the abiding presence of God in your life. However, this process of awareness and where it leads may need a little clarification.

Yielding to the loving search for God requires going through your fears, failures, sins, and every disruptive desire so that you can fully surrender to God and die an all-consuming death to yourself. Contemplation can reveal the deep love of God for each of us, but this love is easily obscured by our attachments and distractions in this life. This isn't the path to living a better story, becoming a better person, or realizing your goals and passions in life. This is a cross to bear and death to endure. You can't half die.

Some days I still catch myself clinging to my old sources of comfort, or the old medicines that I relied on to deal with my anxiety. Zoning out to read sports articles or to scan political news on social media can turn into something far worse than a momentary distraction. It can become an escape plan to run away from reality, to avoid my pain, and to consequently neglect the practices that could lead me into God's life. I know others have turned to sleeping pills, recreational drugs, multiple glasses of wine, or many stiff drinks at the end of the workday to manage the anxiety or pain of life. It's tempting to shuffle the practices that lead to contemplative prayer right into the mix as merely another way to cope with the pain of life. But to do so misunderstands the reason for this type of prayer and its purpose.

Contemplative prayer can have a positive influence on the lives of those who practice it, but any "results" may be described as happy side effects, not the main goal. The main goal is a deeper awareness of and grounding in a divine union with a loving God. The transformation that comes through this union with God will bring greater peace and awareness. But that doesn't guarantee an easy or prosperous life. Rather, the peace that comes may be rooted in an increased acceptance of difficult circumstances. It may be a greater grace to bear with an affliction, like the apostle Paul, who learned that Christ's grace is sufficient for his difficulties. It may look like Julian of Norwich, who experienced visions of Christ's love while nearly dying of a severe sickness.

Although we can't half die to our misguided desires and false selves, the flip side is that we aren't half loved either. Nor are we loved with a string of conditions. If it has been the deepest desire of your heart to be loved by God, then the good news is that God has already demonstrated his love for all of us in this world. God's Spirit has been sent into our world to reveal the gentle, parental heart of God among us.

As an anxious Christian, I have found great relief in contemplative prayer. I have also found that the loving search for God in contemplative prayer is hardly an easy path toward relief for my anxiety, even as contemplation has proven vital in addressing it. I had to go *through* my anxiety, rather than smother it with happy thoughts, positive thinking, or inspirational Bible verses. Thomas Merton writes, "The only trouble is that in the spiritual life there are no tricks and no shortcuts. Those who imagine that they can discover spiritual gimmicks and put them to work for themselves usually ignore God's will and his grace."[1] I have to fully surrender my desires, plans, and misplaced identities to God over and over again. I have to trust that God will one day give me something better if I finally let go of my solutions and goals.

The "results" of contemplative prayer aren't ours to control. This gracious gift of contemplation will surely bring benefits and blessings to our lives, but we shouldn't begin contemplation to reach these kinds of results. In fact, Christians have not practiced contemplation to reach or gain something new. Rather, contemplation connects us with what has always been ours to claim as children of God. Transformation flows out of this new identity grounded in God.

CONTEMPLATION AND DIVINE UNION

As an anxious evangelical Christian, I have struggled to find the right words to write about contemplative prayer. Many Christians begin prayer with the misplaced assumption that God is somehow distant or disconnected from us. Evangelicals have a tendency to take this a step further by anxiously working to prove ourselves committed to or worthy of God's love, attracting the attention of a God who could take us or leave us.

The teachers of contemplative prayer, however, echo the words of Scripture that God's love is already ours, God's presence is already here, and the Holy Spirit has already united God and God's people. Prayer helps us enjoy the reality of divine union with God.

For those whose hearts of stone have been turned into hearts of flesh and who have the promise of the Holy Spirit, the Christian tradition of contemplative prayer does not impart anything new. Martin Laird, a highly regarded contemplative author, writes that contemplative practice "is not a technique but a surrendering of deeply imbedded resistances that allows the sacred within gradually to reveal itself as a simple, fundamental fact."[2] Laird points to the "hidden self" that the Spirit grows in Ephesians 3:16, as well as to God's creative work described in the Psalms: "O Lord, you have searched me and known me. . . . For it was you who formed my inward parts; you knit me together in my mother's womb" (Psalm 139:1, 13). Just as Jesus described himself as the vine and his people as the branches, Paul assures us that our life is hidden in Christ: "For you have died, and your life is hidden with Christ in God. When Christ who is your life is revealed, then you also will be revealed with him in glory" (Colossians 3:3-4). Julian of Norwich wrote, "Prayer is a new, gracious, lasting will of the soul united and fast-bound to the will of God by the precious and mysterious working of the Holy Ghost."[3] Consider the contrast that Thomas Merton sets up between knowledge of God and union with God:

> Hence the aim of meditation, in the context of Christian faith, is not to arrive at an objective and apparently "scientific" knowledge of God, but to come to know him through the

realization that our very being is penetrated with his knowledge and love for us. Our knowledge of God is paradoxically a knowledge not of him as the object of our scrutiny, but of ourselves as utterly dependent on his saving and merciful knowledge of us. It is in proportion as we are known to him that we find our real being and identity in Christ. We know him in and through ourselves in so far as his truth is the source of our being and his merciful love is the very heart of our life and existence. We have no other reason for being, except to be loved by him as our Creator and Redeemer, and to love him in return. There is no true knowledge of God that does not imply a profound grasp and an intimate personal acceptance of this profound relationship.[4]

As we practice contemplative prayer, we will be transformed by the realization of God's love for us. Laird assures us, "Union with God is not something that needs to be acquired but realized . . . it is the realization on this side of death of the fundamental mystery of our existence as the creation of a loving God."[5] He even goes on to say, "God does not know how to be absent."[6]

And so, the "What should we do?" question that comes up with contemplation is a simple act of faith: wait on the Lord and what he has already given to you. God's love and mercy are yours today regardless of how well you deal with distracted thoughts or center on a prayer word. The "results" in the future will most likely look like a greater awareness of God each day and a greater capacity to show love and mercy to others.

The woman who recognized God's love and forgiveness was transformed by God as she responded with gratitude and love: "Therefore, I tell you, her sins, which were many, have been forgiven; hence she has shown great love. But the one to whom little is forgiven, loves little" (Luke 7:47). Those who have known mercy and forgiveness are the ones most likely to show compassion, empathy, and mercy to others. Those who have glimpsed the unfathomable depths of God's love cannot help but respond differently to others in the world. The resulting gift of compassion can place these people in high demand. We want to be held and listened to and cared for by people who have been softened by mercy and grace. Likewise, when we touch the tender mercy of God's loving presence in our lives, we will have a source of life and love that carries more power and strength than all the willpower and obligations we can muster. This life comes out of us like a spring that gushes without end.

We can't control when we will notice God. We can't activate our awareness of God's presence or which aspects of God we will recognize. It may well strike us like a lightning bolt, and we can't plan ahead for how it will transform our lives. Merton was famously compelled to engage with social activism and the issues of his time after he had an epiphany about the love of God while visiting the city of Louisville:

> In Louisville, at the corner of Fourth and Walnut, in the center of the shopping district, I was suddenly overwhelmed with the realization that I loved all these people, that they were mine and I theirs, that we could not be alien to one another even though we were total strangers. . . .
>
> I have the immense joy of being man, a member of a race in which God Himself became incarnate. As if the sorrows and stupidities of the human condition could overwhelm me, now that I realize what we all are. And if only everybody could

realize this! But it cannot be explained. There is no way of telling people that they are all walking around shining like the sun. . . .

Then it was as if I suddenly saw the secret beauty of their hearts, the depths of their hearts where neither sin nor desire nor self-knowledge can reach, the core of their reality, the person that each one is in God's eyes. If only they could all see themselves as they really are. If only we could see each other that way all the time. There would be no more war, no more hatred, no more cruelty, no more greed. . . . But this cannot be seen, only believed and "understood" by a peculiar gift.[7]

CONTEMPLATION SUPPORTS SERVICE

It is surely a risk that those who take the words "flee, be silent, pray" seriously may forget that this posture of silently waiting on God prepares us for ministry and service to others. This is not an invitation to run away from the world for good. The tension over silent prayer and involvement in the day's issues weighed so heavily on Merton's mind after his Louisville epiphany that he wrote a candid letter to Catholic social justice worker Dorothy Day. In it he lamented the resistance of his superiors to his poems and articles addressing nuclear war and other urgent societal issues in the 1960s. "I feel obligated to take very seriously what is going on, and to say whatever my conscience seems to dictate," Merton wrote. "I sometimes wonder if, being in a situation where obedience would completely silence a person on some important moral issue on which others are also keeping silence—a crucial issue like nuclear war—then I would be inclined to wonder if it were not God's will to ask to change my situation."[8]

While Merton added that he had faith God would make a way for him to speak out despite the resistance of his superiors, he didn't back away from the moral obligation to speak up on behalf of his neighbors and all of humanity. "As for writing: I don't feel that I can in conscience, at a time like this, go on writing just about things like meditation, though that has its point," he said. "I think I have to face the big issues, the life-and-death issues: and this is what everyone is afraid of."[9]

Such an exchange is a striking intersection between a pioneer in modern Christian social justice and a pioneer in modern Christian contemplation. While Merton helped revive the practice of contemplation among Christians in the West and continually sought greater solitude in a hermitage later in life, he also felt a strong call to address the issues of his day and to encourage those on the front lines of justice and equality work.

In fact, instead of disconnecting us from the issues of our time, contemplation can give us greater awareness and insight into the false narratives we tell ourselves and the false narratives that drive others. The work of James Baldwin, who has long been one of my favorite writers, remains relevant amid racial injustices today. I have found it particularly revealing that Merton implored his readers to consider Baldwin's *The Fire Next Time*. If they were to read only one book, Merton said, this should be it. He even wrote a bit of fan mail to Baldwin, affirming and encouraging him. Merton added a bit of contemplative perspective on the racial situation in America and the error of white people in particular: "At the heart of the matter then is man's contempt for truth, and the substitution of his 'self' for reality. His image is his truth. He believes in his specter. This is what we are doing, and this is not Christianity or any other genuine religion: it is barbarity."[10]

In such a description of the white resistance to racial and social justice, we see elements of the false self come to the fore. Rather than letting go of the false self and becoming a grain of wheat that dies in the ground in surrender to God's resurrection powers, white people who vilify people of color refuse to acknowledge their own self-deception. In fact, Baldwin acknowledges as much in his book *Notes of a Native Son*: "I imagine one of the reasons people cling to their hates so stubbornly is because they sense, once hate is gone, they will be forced to deal with pain."[11] Having listened to plenty of folks in our current town defending the Confederate monument on the city square and the "heritage" it represents, I have witnessed the power of this false identity firsthand.

Prayer formed a significant foundation of the nonviolent civil rights movement in the 1960s that advocated for equality, justice, and protection under the law. The Alabama Christian Movement for Civil Rights distributed commitment cards that listed ten commandments for the nonviolent movement in Birmingham, Alabama. Those who joined the movement pledged themselves to the following practices and commitments:

1. Meditate daily on the teachings and life of Jesus.

2. Remember always that the non-violent movement seeks justice and reconciliation—not victory.

3. Walk and talk in the manner of love, for God is love.

4. Pray daily to be used by God in order that all men might be free.

5. Sacrifice personal wishes in order that all men might be free.

6. Observe with both friend and foe the ordinary rules of courtesy.

7. Seek to perform regular service for others and for the world.

8. Refrain from the violence of fist, tongue, or heart.

9. Strive to be in good spiritual and bodily health.

10. Follow the directions of the movement and of the captain on a demonstration.[12]

Underneath this list of essential practices, the movement listed practical ways volunteers could help, such as making phone calls, preparing meals, or running errands. Results-oriented, action-loving Christians may be surprised to find that the practical aspects of the movement were tacked on at the bottom of this list. As an anxious evangelical, I would have been eager to prove my commitment and would have flipped the priorities here. But the leaders of the civil rights movement recognized that spiritual formation and soul care precede Spirit-driven action.

While contemplative prayer isn't specifically addressed in this list, the practices that are mentioned—prayer, meditation on the teachings of Jesus, and attention to spiritual health—are tied quite closely to what goes into contemplation. Theologian and contemplative Howard Thurman, who deeply influenced Martin Luther King Jr., speaks directly to the stakes involved when we link contemplation (especially its replacing of the false self with the true self united to God) and activism. Thurman writes, "Anyone who permits another to determine the quality of his inner life gives into the hands of the other the keys to his destiny. If a man knows precisely what he can do to you or what epithet he can hurl against you in order to make you lose your temper, your equilibrium, then he can always keep you under subjection."[13]

The practice of contemplation provides a grounding strength to receive insults that bounce off the true self rooted in God's love. Through contemplative prayer we can be shaped by God's love, increasing our empathy for others and our capacity to love. This can go a long way toward making us peaceful and compassionate even in the most challenging of circumstances.

Contemplative prayer and social justice can sometimes be pitted against each other, and advocates of contemplative prayer and Christians involved in social justice can sometimes misunderstand each other, especially when discussing silence and solitude. Rich Villodas, pastor of New Life Fellowship in Queens, New York, writes, "We need more than ever to cultivate prophetic silence. In so doing we fuel the words we speak with the life and power of God." Elie Wiesel rightly said that "silence encourages the tormentor, never the tormented" in matters of justice and oppression, but regular silence in prayer can ground us and give grace and wisdom to speak effectively. Villodas, who pastors a church in one of America's most diverse zip codes, fuses his contemplative practices with activism and charity, such as sending relief supplies to Puerto Rico after a devastating hurricane and addressing the racial divide in America. Silence in prayer is not the same as and should never lead to silence in causes of equality, justice, or service.[14]

Many Christians involved in advocacy and social justice work today are also leading advocates for contemplative prayer and spiritual formation practices. Jonathan Wilson-Hartgrove, Shane Claiborne, and Enuma Okoro, who are each involved in advocacy and justice work, have compiled a book of daily prayers called *Common Prayer*. Wilson-Hartgrove, a current leader of the Poor People's Campaign, has been involved in the compilation of several books related to the prayer tradition of the church, including *The Wisdom of the Desert Fathers and Mothers* and a paraphrasing of *The Rule of Saint Benedict*, as well as a book detailing the rise of a new monastic movement that incorporates a commitment to serve others and to pray daily in a monastic rhythm. Richard Rohr's Center for Action and Contemplation clearly links the two practices together. And Sister Joan Chittister, best known for her advocacy against the death penalty, has written about the vital place of silence in her own work: "Silence is a frightening thing. Silence leaves us at the mercy of the noise within us. We hear the fears that need to be faced. We hear, then, the angers that need to be cooled. We hear the emptiness that needs to be filled. We hear the cries for humility and reconciliation and centeredness. We hear ambition and arrogance and attitudes of uncaring awash in the shallows of the soul. Silence demands answers. Silence invites us to depth. Silence heals what hoarding and running will not touch."[15]

Such an integration of justice work and prayer continues to grow in new and promising ways. Rohr's Center for Action and Contemplation has created a platform that draws attention to diverse voices addressing a variety of contemplative directions. For instance, significant contributions have already been made by Teresa Pasquale Mateus, a trauma expert and contemplative whose personal mission is to unite contemplation, healing, and action. Along with Jade Perry and Ra Mendoza, Mateus founded the Mystic Soul Project, which aims to "center the voices, wisdom, and identities of [people of color] at the intersections of contemplation, action, and healing."[16] The contemplative tradition has traveled well among diverse peoples and nations historically, and it's my hope that fresh expressions and perspectives on the mysteries of prayer and silence that have emerged will continue to grow.

FINDING OUR CENTER AGAIN

Whether Christians today are just finding their way with contemplative prayer, seeking to apply their compassion and empathy to service and justice, or working on both simultaneously, contemplation ensures that we have a firm foundation in Christ as we show God's compassion and mercy to others. Without the burden of guarding theology or biblical knowledge, we are free to live in and experience the truths of our faith. Building walls of certainty and dogma is a doomed calling, and one at which generations have failed. I have seen one anxious Christian friend after another run empty as they realize that their faith has largely rested on affirming doctrinal statements without a structure of spiritual practices that could keep them grounded before God. One generation after another earnestly studies the Scriptures in search of Jesus, overlooking the fact that Jesus said studying the Scriptures is not the same thing as pursuing him (John 5:39).

Contemplative prayer gives us that path to pursue Jesus and Jesus alone. I haven't had to discard my theological study or my biblical knowledge. The creeds are the same as I found them before I began this journey. The difference is that I'm not asking theology and Bible study to do the things that contemplative prayer can do. Learning and study can be formative and enriching, but they are no substitute for waiting on God in silence alone (Psalm 62:1). Too many evangelicals in my own camp have embraced the former and discarded the latter without investing serious time in it. That isn't to say every Christian must practice contemplative prayer in order to seek God. In fact, some of the most spiritually grounded Christians I know have developed their own spiritual practices. Yet interestingly enough, their spiritual practices often resemble contemplative prayer approaches, such as quietly meditating on Scripture.

Now that we know about Christianity's spiritual heritage that has been lost over time, why wouldn't we embrace it? When I think of the anxiety of Christian spirituality today, especially among evangelicals in America, and its uneasy connections to consumerism and power, I am reminded of how badly we need the wisdom and stability of the contemplative path. Flee, be silent, and pray.

I don't want Christianity in America to collapse or disappear. I want to return to our spiritual roots that keep us grounded in Christ. Our spiritual heritage is made up of women and men who fled to quiet, secret places, silenced themselves before God, and prayed. In the silence of these lonely places, they found God's heartbeat of love for them and for the rest of the world. This love transformed them. When the distraught, hopeless, or confused people of nearby cities hit rock bottom, some turned to these women and men, who had resolved to lose by every measure of earthly success and progress so that they could gain the deeper things of God.

MAKING SPACE TO PRAY

Throughout my jam-packed days, I can still become a bit like a meteorite crashing into earth. Running from one task to another, I may only come to a flaming stop as I hit the ground of my prayer practices. If I've been moving at full speed all day without mindfulness of God or the state of my own soul, stopping for contemplation or any other prayer becomes a jarring collision. When contemplative prayer is my first break all day, I shouldn't be surprised that it's hard to settle down or to rest before God. Mind you, that doesn't mean I've "failed" at prayer. Rather, my soul is recovering or settling down from my anxiety, activity, and many, many thoughts.

Once I made centering prayer a regular practice, however, I began to notice that I'm not always at the mercy of my circumstances or emotions. The practice of "letting my thoughts go" in centering prayer has helped me become a little more detached from my own thinking. Just as the larger Christian movement in the United States generally needs to examine its relationship with power, cultural influence, and the influence of systematic theological certainty, individual Christians also need to let go of our need to control and manage our encounters with God.

Outside of longer contemplative stretches, I have started to seize quiet moments to practice contemplative prayer throughout the day, such as when I'm working on a simple task. The desert fathers and mothers practiced contemplation while working with their hands as they wove baskets or tended their gardens. They dedicated time to pray, but they also saw their daily tasks as an opportunity to be present for God. You could say that they became addicted to silence, while our culture has become addicted to noise, distraction, and entertainment.

There are opportunities for silence and contemplation beyond dedicated prayer time, provided that we embrace the possibilities of silence. For instance, I have learned to love silence while doing the dishes, especially if I check in on my soul and find that I'm like a meteor streaking toward the earth. When Thomas Merton joined his Cistercian monastery, he found that prayer and work were tied together. He quips in *The Seven*

Storey Mountain about his days swinging an ax and saying "All for Jesus!" through gritted teeth.

FINDING HOPE IN GOD'S MERCY

If the recent history of Christianity in America has taught me anything, it's that we would all do well to pray, "Lord, have mercy on me, a sinner." That's one prayer from the Bible that we all should feel comfortable repeating daily. This simple prayer puts us in our place and acknowledges God's great mercy for us.

When I feel lost, without hope or a path forward, I remember these simple words: flee, be silent, pray. In many ways, the evangelical movement I know in America has spiritually burned out, and the movement primarily continues through the will of leaders, institutions, and a collective fear that God isn't real. There are plenty of challenges among mainline Protestant denominations and the Catholic Church as well. Is there any hope for our distracted, defiant church today? Should we even bother sitting in silence if so many churches are really fueled by wielding power and generating noise? Can we take a step forward by first learning how to retreat?

I believe we can find hope in the silence of surrender before God. We need resurrection, and that's what God specializes in doing for the hopeless and seemingly dead. The one catch is that we have to let go. We have to let go of our power, control, and plans for the future. We have to admit that we are empty and to face the bitter howls of the darkness. Our worst fears may be realized, but not forever.

In the silence and seeming emptiness, there is a light, perhaps faint at first. Perhaps the light won't appear in a way that we are expecting. There, where all appears lost, we will begin to find the mystery of God with us. In solitude and silence, we can begin to recover what it means to pray and to finally rest in the peace of God's loving presence.

PRACTICING THE PRACTICE

This book weaves my own story of finding contemplative prayer with a very basic introduction to several spiritual practices that have helped in my loving search for God. I never set out to write the definitive book on contemplative prayer by any means, and I'm always happy to recommend other books, especially the titles that follow in the "Recommended Reading" section.

If you're looking for an excellent next step in practicing contemplative prayer, I highly recommend Martin Laird's accessible book *Into the Silent Land*. It even comes with the informal stamp of approval from several monks at Thomas Merton's Abbey of Gethsemani.

Recommended Reading

I could name books related to contemplative prayer all day, but for the practical purpose of helping readers take a next step in their journeys, I'll begin by saying that many excellent websites and resources can be easily found online. For instance:

- Look for YouTube videos by Cynthia Bourgeault, Thomas Keating, and Richard Rohr.
- The website ContemplativeOutreach.org has many resources for prayer.
- You can find a basic Examen at the Ignatian Spirituality website: www.ignatianspirituality.com/ignatian-prayer/the-examen.
- *The Spark My Muse* podcast by Lisa Colón DeLay has a variety of guests, and many have a contemplative perspective to share.

As for a simple starting point for most readers who are new to contemplative prayer, I recommend the following books:

Into the Silent Land by Martin Laird

The Inner Experience by Thomas Merton

Highly instructive books that offer a deeper dive into contemplative prayer include the following:

Centering Prayer and Inner Awakening by Cynthia Bourgeault

Open Mind, Open Heart by Thomas Keating

Contemplative Prayer by Thomas Merton

New Seeds of Contemplation by Thomas Merton

Everything Belongs by Richard Rohr

The Way of the Heart by Henri J. M. Nouwen

Spiritual classics that address contemplation:

The Cloud of Unknowing (translated by Carmen Acevedo Butcher)

The Interior Castle by Teresa of Ávila

Contemporary nonfiction that explores contemplative practices:

Mystics and Misfits by Christiana N. Peterson

Coming Clean by Seth Haines

Found by Micha Boyett

Glory Happening by Kaitlin Curtice

A Beautiful Disaster by Marlena Graves

Acknowledgments

When I released the first edition of this book, I genuinely wondered if anyone would read the story of an anxious evangelical learning contemplative prayer from a bunch of Catholics. To my pleasant surprise, the early readers of *Flee, Be Silent, Pray* were enthusiastic about this book. Just a few of many (I'm sorry I can't mention you all!) include Lisa Burgess, Glynn Young, Jason Freyer, and Sarah Porto, and there were many others from my newsletter list who read the first edition and offered timely feedback. It was their encouragement and support that kept me going through the finishing touches and release. I can't even begin to name all the readers who wrote reviews, shared about it on social media, or wrote notes to me about the book. I'm grateful for your generosity and kindness. I never take a single email, review, or comment from you for granted.

Throughout the process of working on the first edition and this newly revised edition, the encouragement of fellow writers, including Tara Owens, Christie Purifoy, Sarah Bessey, Anne Bogel, Tsh Oxenreider, Holly Rankin Zaher, Andi Cumbo-Floyd, Addie Zierman, Emily P. Freeman, Michelle DeRusha, Micha Boyett, Shawn Smucker, and Lisa Delay (among many, many others), has been vital for sustaining me. I continued through many difficult days knowing that they too were committed to the deep work of writing to serve their readers. A timely email from Seth Haines may be one of the main reasons why I persevered with this project in the first place. The wisdom and instruction of the people at Central Vineyard in Columbus, Ohio, was foundational in my pursuit of contemplative prayer.

As for the current edition of this book, a fortuitous snowstorm in Grand Rapids and the timely support of Seth Haines and Shawn Smucker played crucial roles. Seth and Shawn have steadfastly believed in my writing and this project in particular. I can't imagine embarking on this journey without their wisdom and encouragement.

Amy Gingerich at Herald Press was attentive and encouraging right from the start. Valerie Weaver-Zercher literally organized my thoughts better than I could—which is the highest praise I can think of for an editor. This book is far clearer and better organized because of her diligent work.

My family has played a crucial role in supporting me through prayer (intercession, deliverance . . . you name it, they've prayed it). My wife Julie has stood with me through the highs and lows of my journey through anxiety, contemplative prayer, and book publishing. Anxiety can be isolating and discouraging, and anxious Christians who offer anxious prayers need love and security to thrive. She has been by my side to listen through the hard times and to support my pursuit of mental and spiritual health.

Also, strange as it is to thank a dead man, Thomas Merton, you loved Jesus, you were a mess at times, and you wrote *all of it down* as your gift and ministry to the world. Thank you for telling us that paradise is all around us, the sword is gone, and that we are indeed shining like the sun in the glow of the Father's love.

Notes

Chapter 1: Say Goodbye

1   Thomas Merton, *Thoughts in Solitude* (New York: Farrar, Straus and Giroux, 1999), 82.

2   Quoted in Henry L. Carrigan Jr., trans., *The Wisdom of the Desert Fathers and Mothers* (Brewster, MA: Paraclete Press, 2010), 93.

3   Henri J. M. Nouwen, *The Way of the Heart: Connecting with God through Prayer, Wisdom, and Silence* (New York: Seabury, 1981), 15.

Chapter 2: Start at Love

1   Thomas Merton, *No Man Is an Island* (New York: Mariner Books, 2002), 17–18.

2   Richard Rohr, *Everything Belongs: The Gift of Contemplative Prayer*, rev. ed. (New York: Crossroad Publishing, 2003), 69.

3   Ibid., 20.

4   François Fénelon, "The Sacrifice of Love," in *100 Days in the Secret Place: Classic Writings from Madame Guyon, François Fénelon, and Michael Molinos on the Deeper Christian Life*, comp. Gene Edwards (Shippensburg, PA: Destiny Image, 2015), 11.

Chapter 3: Pray with Scripture

1   For more about the history of fixed-hour prayer and the origins of *The Divine Hours* by Phyllis Tickle, see an excerpt from *The Divine Hours: Prayers for Summertime* at Phyllis Tickle, "A Brief History of Fixed-Hour Prayer," Explore Faith, accessed August 9, 2018, http://explorefaith.org/prayer/prayer/fixed/a_brief_history.php.

2   Thomas Merton, *Thoughts in Solitude* (New York: Farrar, Straus and Giroux, 1999), 46–47.

3   James Martin, SJ, *Together on Retreat* (San Francisco: HarperOne, 2013), Sec. 549.

Chapter 4: Cheat at Prayer

1   Phyllis Tickle, *The Divine Hours: Prayers for Springtime* (New York: Random House, 2001), 548.
2   "Other Prayers," Vineyard Church Ann Arbor, accessed August 30, 2018, http://annarborvineyard.org/getting-connected/ spiritual-formation/other-prayers. This prayer is often attributed to Desmond Tutu and considered by some to be adapted from an original prayer by Sir Francis Drake.
3   "You Have Prepared in Peace the Path" in *An African Prayer Book*, comp. Desmond Tutu (New York: Doubleday, 1995), 119.
4   "Other Prayers," Vineyard Church Ann Arbor. A prayer by Saint Ignatius of Loyola.
5   Phyllis Tickle, *The Divine Hours: Prayers for Summertime* (New York: Random House, 2000), 171.
6   Ibid., 567.
7   Ibid., 444.
8   Tickle, *The Divine Hours: Prayers for Springtime*, 658.
9   Tickle, *The Divine Hours: Prayers for Summertime*, 183.
10 Thomas Merton, *The Wisdom of the Desert*, rev. ed. (New York: New Directions, 1970), 105.
11 Tickle, *The Divine Hours: Prayers for Springtime*, 566.

Chapter 5: Don't Forget to Be Mindful

1   Richard Rohr, *Falling Upward: A Spirituality for the Two Halves of Life* (San Francisco: Jossey-Bass, 2011), 74.
2   Thomas Merton, *No Man Is an Island* (New York: Mariner Books, 2002), 32.
3   Ibid.
4   Thomas Merton, *Thoughts in Solitude* (New York: Farrar, Straus and Giroux, 1999), 40.
5   Richard Rohr, *Breathing Under Water: Spirituality and the Twelve Steps* (Cincinnati, OH: St. Anthony Messenger Press, 2011), xxiii.
6   Richard Rohr, *Everything Belongs: The Gift of Contemplative Prayer*, rev. ed. (New York: Crossroad Publishing, 2003), 43.

Chapter 6: Retreat

1   Henri J. M. Nouwen, *The Way of the Heart: Connecting with God through Prayer, Wisdom, and Silence* (New York: Seabury, 1981), 26.

2   Ibid., 28.

3   Ibid., 25.

4   Henri J. M. Nouwen, *Out of Solitude: Three Meditations on the Christian Life* (Notre Dame, IN: Ave Maria, 1974), 45.

5   Brennan Manning, *Abba's Child: The Cry of the Heart for Intimate Belonging* (Colorado Springs: NavPress, 2015), 39–40.

6   John Chryssavgis, *In the Heart of the Desert: The Spirituality of the Desert Fathers and Mothers* (Bloomington, IN: World Wisdom, 2008), 17.

7   Nouwen, *The Way of the Heart*, 37.

8   Thomas Merton, *The Seven Storey Mountain* (New York: Mariner Books, 1999), 410.

9   Thomas Merton, *The Wisdom of the Desert*, rev. ed. (New York: New Directions, 1970), 168.

10 Ibid., 25.

11 Ibid., 25–26.

12 Thomas Merton, *Thoughts in Solitude* (New York: Farrar, Straus and Giroux, 1999), 96.

13 Ibid., 5.

Chapter 7: Be Quiet

1   Henri J. M. Nouwen, *The Way of the Heart: Connecting with God through Prayer, Wisdom, and Silence* (New York: Seabury, 1981), 54.

2   Thomas Merton, *Thoughts in Solitude* (New York: Farrar, Straus and Giroux, 1999), 2.

3   Nouwen, *The Way of the Heart*, 58.

4   KJ Dell'Antonia, "Does Texting at a Stop Sign Count?" *New York Times*, March 19, 2014, https://parenting.blogs.nytimes.com/2014/03/19/does-texting-at-a-stop-sign-count/.

5   Thomas Merton, *No Man Is an Island* (New York: Mariner Books, 2002), 33.

6   Thomas Merton, *The Wisdom of the Desert*, rev. ed. (New York: New Directions, 1970), 14.

7   Quoted in Henry L. Carrigan Jr., trans., *The Wisdom of the Desert Fathers and Mothers* (Brewster, MA: Paraclete Press, 2010), 128.

8   Richard Rohr, "Spirituality of Letting Go: Week 2," Richard Rohr's Daily Meditations, Center for Action and Contemplation, September 6, 2016, http://thecenterforactionandcontemplation .cmail20.com/t/ViewEmail/d/5C440506F204AF50/ BC627013C23971D8D9767B6002735221.

9   Merton, *The Wisdom of the Desert*, 22.

Chapter 8: Begin with Intention

1   Thomas Merton, *The Inner Experience: Notes on Contemplation* (San Francisco: Harper Collins, 2003), 2.

2   Thomas Keating, foreword to *Centering Prayer and Inner Awakening*, by Cynthia Bourgeault (Chicago: Cowley Publications, 2004), vii.

3   Cynthia Bourgeault, *Centering Prayer and Inner Awakening* (Chicago: Cowley Publications, 2004), 5.

4   Ibid., 22.

5   *The Cloud of Unknowing*, trans. Ira Progoff (New York: Delta Books: 1957), 76.

6   Bourgeault, *Centering Prayer and Inner Awakening*, 6

7   Martin Laird, *Into the Silent Land: A Guide to the Christian Practice of Contemplation* (New York: Oxford, 2006), 42.

8   Bourgeault, *Centering Prayer and Inner Awakening*, 30.

9   Henri J. M. Nouwen, *Out of Solitude: Three Meditations on the Christian Life* (Notre Dame, IN: Ave Maria, 1974), 21.

10 Michael Molinos, "A Commitment Established," in *100 Days in the Secret Place: Classic Writings from Madame Guyon, François Fénelon, and Michael Molinos on the Deeper Christian Life*, comp. Gene Edwards (Shippensburg, PA: Destiny Image, 2015), 21.

11 William Meninger, *The Loving Search for God: Contemplative Prayer and The Cloud of Unknowing* (New York, NY: Continuum, 1998), 14–15.

12 Mike McHargue ("Science Mike") and Michael Gungor, "The Cosmic Christ with Richard Rohr," April 11, 2016, in *The Liturgists Podcast*, 1:05:51, http://www.theliturgists.com/podcast/2016/4/12/ episode-35-the-cosmic-christ-with-richard-rohr.

Chapter 9: Accept Mystery

1   Richard Rohr, *Everything Belongs: The Gift of Contemplative Prayer*, rev. ed. (New York: Crossroad Publishing, 2003), 46–47.

2   Thomas Merton, *No Man Is an Island* (New York: Mariner Books, 2002), 32.

3   Cynthia Bourgeault, *Centering Prayer and Inner Awakening* (Chicago: Cowley Publications, 2004), 24–25.

4   Robert Inchausti, ed., *Echoing Silence: Thomas Merton on the Vocation of Writing* (Boston: New Seeds, 2007), 22–23.

5   Brennan Manning, *Abba's Child: The Cry of the Heart for Intimate Belonging* (Colorado Springs: NavPress, 2015), 23.

6   Inchausti, *Echoing Silence*, 23.

7   See Chuck DeGroat, "3 Truths About the 'Dark Night of the Soul,'" *Christianity Today*, February 2015, http://www.christianitytoday .com/pastors/2015/february-online-only/3-truths-of-dark-night-of -soul.html.

8   Thomas Merton, *The Inner Experience: Notes on Contemplation* (San Francisco: HarperCollins, 2003), 16.

9   Mother Teresa, *Come Be My Light: The Private Writings of the "Saint of Calcutta,"* ed. Brian Kolodiejchuk (New York: Doubleday, 2007), 208.

10 Teresa of Ávila, *The Interior Castle*, trans. E. Allison Peers (New York: Doubleday, 1972), 191.

11 François Fénelon, "Embracing the Cross," in *100 Days in the Secret Place: Classic Writings from Madame Guyon, François Fénelon, and Michael Molinos on the Deeper Christian Life*, ed. Gene Edwards (Shippensburg, PA: Destiny Image, 2015), 1.

12 Ibid., 11.

13 Emily Stimpson Chapman, "Understanding the 'dark night of the soul,'" *OSV Newsweekly*, May 20, 2015, https://www.osv.com/ OSVNewsweekly/Story/TabId/2672/ArtMID/13567/ ArticleID/17512/Understanding-the-dark-night-of-the-soul.

14 Richard Rohr, *Immortal Diamond: The Search for Our True Self* (San Francisco: Jossey-Bass, 2013), 36–37.

15 Manning, *Abba's Child*, 25.

16 Chapman, "Understanding the Dark Night."

17 Rohr, *Everything Belongs*, 46.

Chapter 10: Now What?

1 Thomas Merton, *Contemplative Prayer* (New York: Image Books, 1969), 13.

2 Martin Laird, *Into the Silent Land: A Guide to the Christian Practice of Contemplation* (New York: Oxford, 2006), 8.

3 Julian of Norwich, *Revelations of Divine Love*, trans. Barry Windeatt (Oxford: Oxford University Press, 2015), 92.

4 Merton, *Contemplative Prayer*, 61.

5 Laird, *Into the Silent Land*, 10.

6 Ibid., 15.

7 Thomas Merton, *Conjectures of a Guilty Bystander* (New York: Image Books, 1965), 153–55.

8 Robert Inchausti, ed., *Echoing Silence: Thomas Merton on the Vocation of Writing* (Boston: New Seeds, 2007), 179–180.

9 Ibid., 180.

10 Ibid., 128.

11 James Baldwin, *Notes of a Native Son* (Boston: Beacon Press, 1955), 101.

12 "Commitment Card," Teaching American History, accessed August 30, 2018, http://teachingamericanhistory.org/library/document/commitment-card/.

13 Howard Thurman, *Jesus and the Disinherited* (Boston: Beacon Press, 1996), 28.

14 Rich Villodas, "Silence: The Unexpected, Prophetic Starting Point for Social Justice," *Missio Alliance*, November 2, 2016, https://www.missioalliance.org/silence-unexpected-prophetic-starting-point-justice.

15 Joan D. Chittister, OSB, *Wisdom Distilled from the Daily: Living the Rule of St. Benedict Today*, repr. ed. (San Francisco: HarperSanFranciso, 2009), 169.

16 "Teresa Pasquale Mateus '15 Alumni Spotlight," Center for Action and Contemplation, May 23, 2017, https://cac.org/teresa-pasquale-mateus-15-2017-05-23/.

The Author

ED CYZEWSKI is the author of *A Christian Survival Guide, Coffeehouse Theology*, and other books. His writing has appeared in *Christianity Today* and *Leadership Journal*, and he blogs regularly at Patheos. Cyzewski founded The Contemplative Writer website and leads contemplative prayer retreats. Cyzewski has a master of divinity from Biblical Theological Seminary in Philadelphia and works as a freelance writer and editor. He and his wife have three children. Connect with him at EdCyzewski.com.